Portrait of a Middle-Class Negro Family

AT THE EDGE OF HARLEM

photographs by Edward Lettau
text by Edward Wakin

William Morrow & Company   New York, 1965

This book originated in an idea by Photographer Edward Lettau for a television documentary that received a Freedoms Foundation Award. Produced by the National Council of Catholic Men in association with the American Broadcasting Company and written by Dennis Clark, the documentary was entitled "The Children's Choice" for the program series, "Directions '63 . . . A Catholic Perspective." Some of Mr. Lettau's pictures for the program are used in this book with the permission of the American Broadcasting Company.

Contents

This book is about a single American family, the Crearys of New York City. The location is significant because it is in Harlem. So is the color of their skin, as far as white America is concerned. The Crearys look upon themselves primarily as Americans, Christians, and parents; also as voters, TV viewers, shoppers, newspaper readers, moviegoers. But color casts a cruel shadow on what otherwise would be a familiar middle-class life.

Unlike the downtrodden Negro who has become a well-known statistic, the Crearys have an immediate future. Poised at the edge of Harlem—both physically and psychologically—they are ready to leave. That is why we introduce them. They will be the first to move next door or to sit at the next desk. Steadily, unavoidably, and with the friendliest intentions, the Crearys and other Negroes like them are moving closer to white America, hoping that white America is ready to accept them.

Kenneth 8   Martin 5   Joseph 6   Audrey

John   Rose 1   Eve 4   Marianne 9

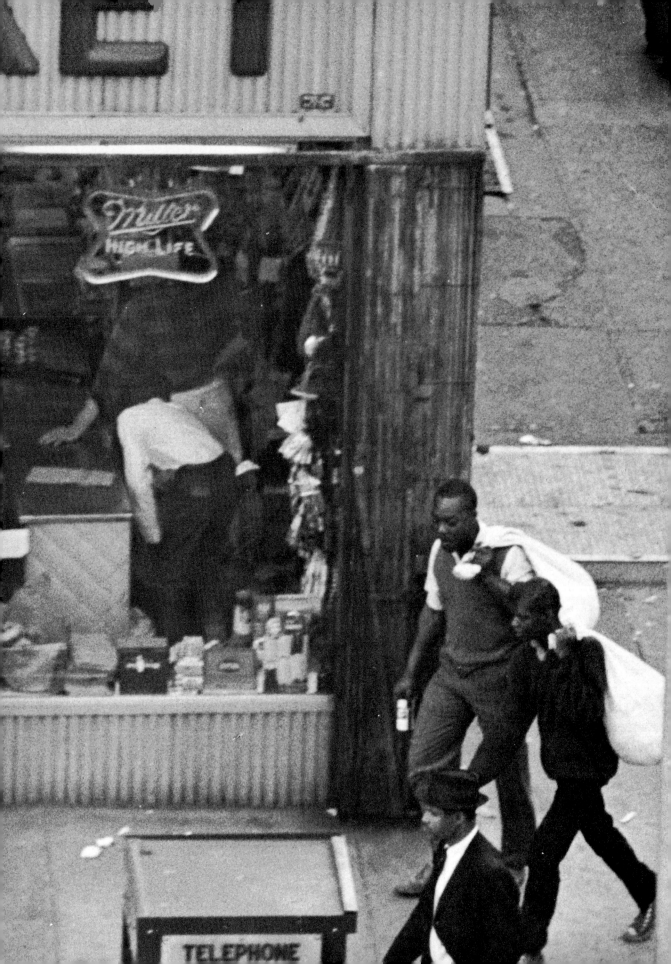

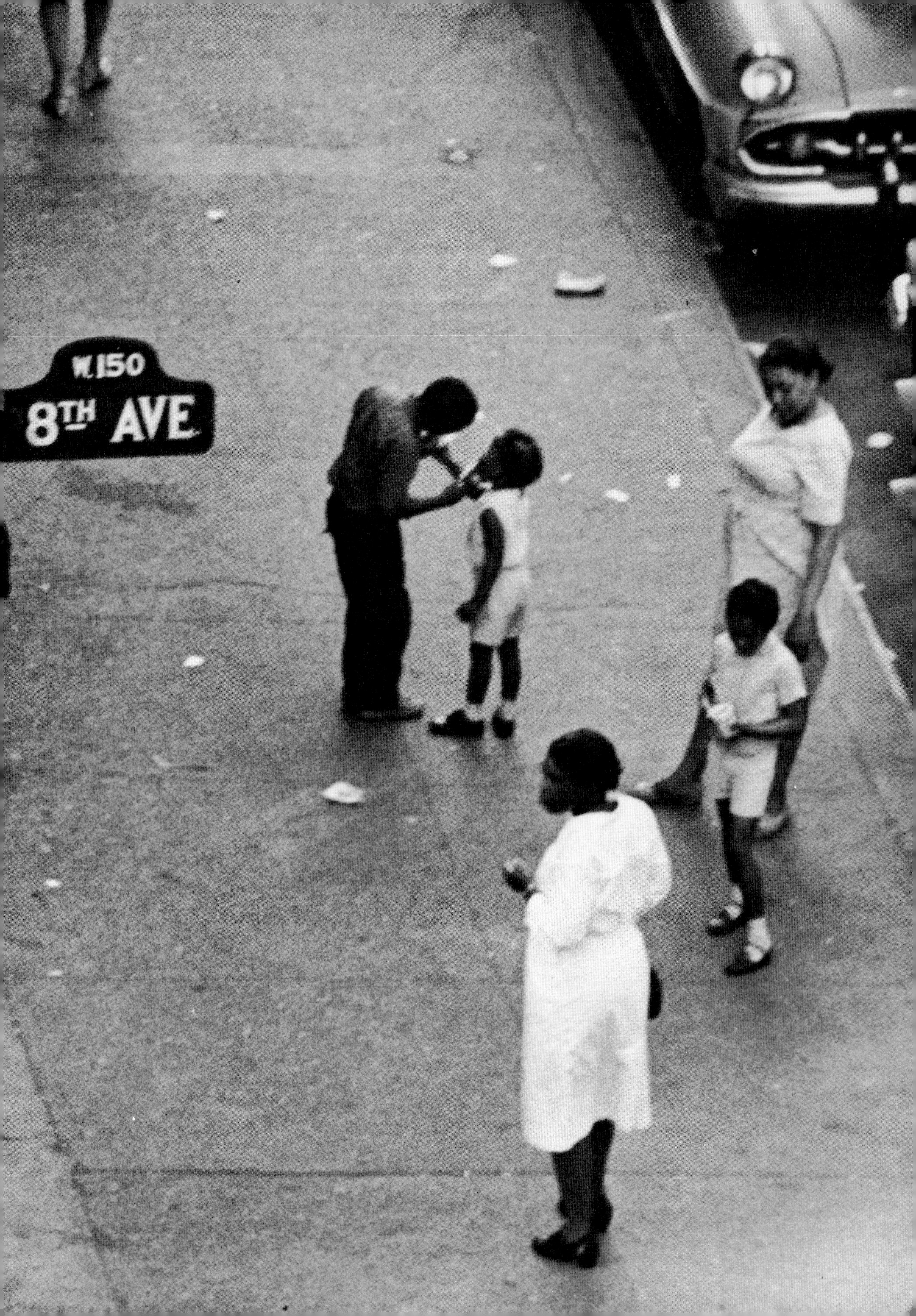
W.150
8TH AVE

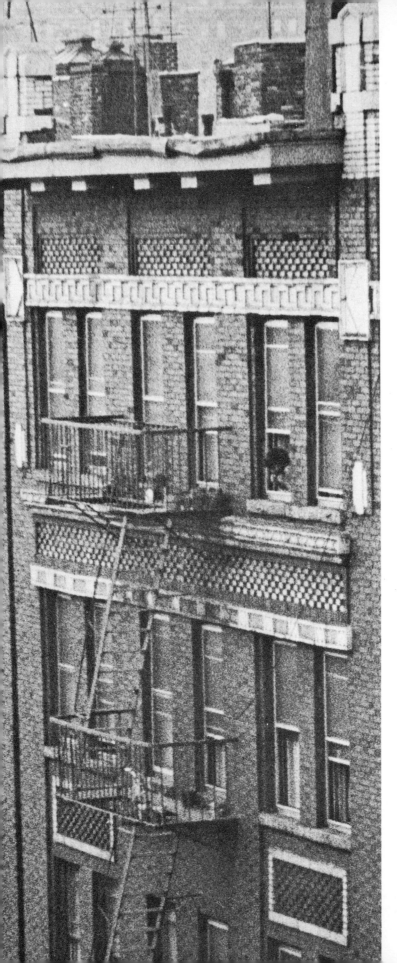

At five o'clock Friday morning, rising an hour earlier than usual, Herman John Creary looked out his fourth-floor bedroom window. Across Seventh Avenue, he could see the lines of idle trains in the IRT subway yards next to the Harlem River and the highway by it. Train yards and highways as well as rivers are distinctive boundaries for Negro ghettos, man providing where God has not wrought. Visible across the river in the Bronx were the County Jail, the County Courthouse, the Bronx Terminal Market, and, to the north, the top of the Yankee Stadium.

On the sidewalk below, police chalk lines reminded Herman John Creary of the recent evening when his eight-year-old son, Kenneth, looked out the same window and saw a man lying on the ground. He ran to his mother, shouting "There's a dead man on the sidewalk." Although she wouldn't listen, he was right. The man was a drug addict who had collapsed and died in front of their building. After the police had marked the spot with chalk lines, Kenneth went around the house saying, "I told you so." The incident was not surprising; the center of Harlem's drug traffic is only a few blocks away.

For the Crearys and their six children, home is in the northeast corner of the Dunbar Apartments, a block-square quadrangle of buildings. Inside the main archway, the tenants are listed alphabetically; each of them is a middle-class holdout resisting deprivation at the edge of Harlem. On the opposite wall is a red-and-blue mailbox and an honor roll of Dunbar residents who left their ghetto to die for their country.

"Moving here in August 1958, was like coming home again—reluctantly," Audrey Creary said. "I grew up in the Dunbar Apartments in Harlem and the associations weren't pleasant. But the rent was low for six rooms ($102) and we had to get out of the place we rented in the Bronx. The rent was high and the place was not being kept up. It was a changing neighborhood that had all sorts of problems, and then, to top it off, John got into an argument with the landlord. We had to move, and so when the doctor told my mother the four flights were too much for her heart, we took over this apartment."

Dunbar had changed since Audrey was a child. Built by the Rockefeller family at a cost of $3.5 million, as one of the first large housing developments, Dunbar's nine six-story buildings were opened in 1928 and many members of the Negro elite moved in. Nowadays, the tone is more respectable than stylish. Like the bank clerk who must wear his white shirt two days running, it is straining to keep up appearances. Audrey can compare past and present.

"When I was growing up here, there were no wire fences around the grass, and there were even flowers. We used to live on the first floor, and my mother would watch my brother and me play. In 1953, I moved in again with my parents. They had moved to this apartment and John was on temporary duty overseas with the Air Force. I taught school and lived in what is now our bedroom and the boys' bedroom, with the bathroom in between. It was an apartment within an apartment and the only time I lived in Harlem without being cramped. The view from Seventh Avenue was really exciting then. There was no highway to block the river, and I used to delight in the way the sun glistened off the water. You could forget Harlem."

Because it looks away from Harlem, the view from Seventh Avenue has always been prized. On Eighth Avenue, it is impossible to ignore the harsh realities of Harlem life: the noise, the roaring arguments, the prostitutes, the pushers, the sirens, the nighttime screams—all the jarring reminders that Harlem dwarfs other ghettos in size, sin, and human spoilage.

The Seventh Avenue view matches the outlook of the Crearys, who look, travel, play, study, plan, and dream outward, as they say repeatedly. While they live at the edge of Harlem physically, psychologically they are on the other side of the river. They exemplify the North's emergent Negro middle class, which frees itself from the ghetto mentality long before it moves next door to a white family.

The Crearys can walk many bridges out of the introverted Harlem life that envelops lower-class Negroes because education, income, and occupation have led to increasing contacts with the outside white world. The Crearys enjoy growing acceptance and are passing on their feelings of acceptance to their children. The children, in turn, can move into the white world with greater personal ease to match their increasing access.

In their daily and weekend pattern of living, the Crearys escape from and return to the demoralizing apartness that poisons ghetto life in America. Each new venture and each new bridge into the surrounding white world is constantly threatened by insult and insolence, by rebuff and rejection. When rejection takes place amid the surface racial acceptance of the North, it is not mercifully clear-cut, but is frequently ambiguous. The gnawing uncertainty is expressed in the question that Audrey often can't help but ask herself, "Was it because . . . OR BECAUSE?"

On that Friday morning, John (as his family and friends call him) used his early-morning head start to grade the French exercises of his students at William L. Ettinger Junior High School 13 in East Harlem. He also revised an article on interracial marriage. At about six o'clock, Audrey began her morning preparations by taking down the clothes hanging in the kitchen. Since she doesn't feel safe using the clothes line on the apartment roof, she usually hangs her daily washing indoors. Next, Marianne, who sleeps in the living room with Eve, woke up, followed by the three boys. The boys share one bedroom, which has a double-decker and a single bed. Audrey's cousin, a New York Sanitation worker, lives in the third bedroom and contributes toward the rent.

During the morning commotion of trips to the two small bathrooms and of searches for clothing and schoolbooks, breakfast was eaten in stages, with Marianne and Kenneth fixing the eggs. John ate and hurried Marianne along so they could leave by seven-thirty for the predominantly white Mt. St. Ursula Academy in the Bronx. The first of the children to be transplanted from Harlem, Marianne, a fifth grader, was sent to the academy in the middle of the third grade when the Crearys became dissatisfied with her teacher.

The boys attended Resurrection parochial school nearby, where their mother can recall her own schooldays in Harlem. "I remember that my first-grade class came to a stop each time a dynamite blast was set off by construction work for the low-income Harlem River Houses across the street. At that time, a few white families were still in the neighborhood and I remember having a fight and going home from school in tears when I was called 'black' for the first time.

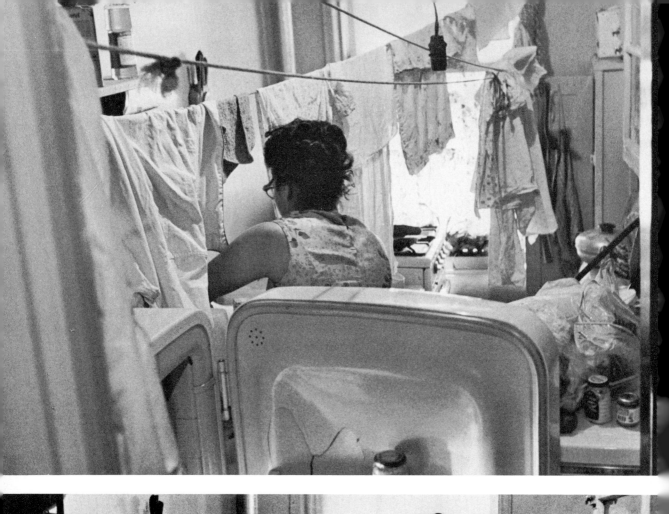

"In those days, the Negroes were 'brainwashed.' They took second-class status for granted. The teachers used to call lateness CPT (Colored People's Time). And they used to say 'you people.' Once, in the fourth grade, my teacher told the class about the remark made by the white custodian when a Christmas crèche was set up and the Negro wise man was placed looking away from baby Jesus. 'That's just the way they are,' he said. The teacher thought it was a funny remark worth telling her Negro pupils."

Audrey also became aware of color bigotry among Negroes, and she recalls the cruel rhyme of her childhood: "If you're white, you're all right. If you're yellow, you're mellow. If you're brown, stick aroun'. If you're black, step back." She adds, "That little thing went on through the race until recently. Now you wouldn't dare say anything like that. Now if you're black, so much the better."

At present, the student body at Resurrection is overwhelmingly Negro with a few Puerto Ricans. Resurrection's teachers are haphazardly integrated: two Negro lay teachers, one Negro nun, and the rest, white nuns. Before leaving for the school, the Creary boys made their beds and cleared the breakfast table. They were out of the house by eight-thirty, Kenneth to the third grade where he was taught by the Negro nun, Joseph to the first grade, and Martin to kindergarten. They are never late for school.

After driving north along the Major Deegan Expressway to the Van Cortlandt Park exit, John deposited Marianne at her school by eight o'clock, the first pupil to arrive. He reached his junior high school on 106th Street, between Madison and Park avenues, by eight-fifteen, squeezed his 1958 Rambler station wagon into a parking place, and strode through the school lobby. Student signs for approaching school elections reflected the Puerto Rican–Negro mixture of the student body: "For a zooming G.O. Vote for Anna Lopez." "All the girls are screaming Reinaldo Ortiz's name. If he's elected president, he'll bring our school tremendous fame." "Vote for Moore and Ettinger won't be a Bore." "To serve all my fellow students is one of my highest ambitions—Esther for Treasurer."

After punching the school's time clock, John picked up the *New York Times* from his mailbox and greeted a Negro teacher (who is married to an Irish Catholic) and a white social studies teacher whom he usually joins for lunch. He walked upstairs to Room 418 and, in preparation for the arrival of the students at eight-forty, he set up a tape recorder and record player he uses for French classes. Partly as a tranquilizer and partly to fill the cultural gap, John plays classical records as the pupils settle down. That morning in East Harlem, the class arrived to the strains of Liszt's "Concerto Pathetique."

Although John's eighth-grade boys and girls entered with a rush, they were well behaved and surprisingly well dressed for a junior high school in a depressed, run-down neighborhood. In fact, it is a commonplace observation among the teachers that many pupils spend too much on clothes. Drawing its 1,500 pupils from an area reaching from Third to Fifth avenues and from East 102nd to East 115th streets, the school serves concentrated pockets of Negroes and Puerto Ricans.

Both school and neighborhood reflect the rehabilitation efforts of the city. Housing projects are replacing tenements, and a new junior high school replaced dilapidated premises in 1959. School authorities then changed the name from Patrick Henry to William L. Ettinger, a New York City school superintendent from 1918 to 1924.

The school is ostentatiously committed to the care and preparation of boys and girls for the middle class, and they have at hand the most obvious examples in their teachers. The school's location in a trouble area earns it the euphemistic label of Special Service School and, indeed, Ettinger Junior High is the very model of a progressive problem school in a downtrodden metropolitan area. A Higher Horizons program of counseling and culture strains to raise student levels. Open Enrollment permits students to transfer to less segregated schools. An extensive remedial reading program is aided by volunteers who tutor backward students. Even orientation works in both directions: English for the Spanish-speaking students and a special familiarization course for new teachers. Each grade level has its own band and its own orchestra as part of an energetic music program.

A Career Guidance Program pinpoints potential dropouts and tries to keep them in school with vocational training. Free dental care is provided two days a week at a nearby clinic, and a dental team sweeps through the school once a year to give every pupil a dental check-up. And, to cope with the neighborhood's high incidence of TB, every pupil is X-rayed annually. For those in need — forty percent of the school — free lunches are provided.

This conscientious welfarism under the direction of Principal Bernard Weiss extended the middle-class ideal to such requirements as wearing a tie to school and—at the weekly assembly—a white shirt as well.

Shortly before nine, the voice of Principal Weiss was piped into all classrooms over the loudspeaker system. In a daily ritual that followed attendance-taking and announcements, Principal Weiss intoned the Pledge of Allegiance and the fourth stanza of "America the Beautiful." Then, he berated chronic latecomers, reminding teachers and pupils that "reduction of lateness is a major school goal." He explained: "To develop as responsible persons, you must learn to get to work on time, and school is your work. . . . But, we don't want to scold the whole school for the malfeasance of a few." (At this point, John Creary wrote the word, malfeasance, on the board in his classroom and noted, "That's a new word for you.") Principal Weiss reminded the pupils of an afternoon assembly featuring a musician from Lincoln Center and of the need for proper dress. He also mentioned the afternoon meeting of the Homework Club for students who have no place at home to do schoolwork or who want to work under the supervision of teacher volunteers.

At nine, the students lined up at the classroom door and waited for Teacher Creary's send-off to their various classes, "Start out and have a good day." For him, the morning in Room 418 consisted of an unassigned first period devoted to administrative details and classroom preparation, followed by eighth-grade French, supplementary English, ninth-grade French, and lunch from eleven fifty-three to twelve thirty-eight. John, who has his teaching license in French, also teaches English, since the school's language program is not yet large enough for a full teaching assignment in French.

Principal Weiss, who described John as "one of the best French teachers in the city," hired him as a regular substitute teacher in September 1960, when the school became coeducational and expanded in size. For most of the previous school year, John had taught at another Harlem school, but left because he did not have enough opportunity to teach French. As a substitute teacher, he could pick his school, a privilege that he lost when he became a regular teacher. His annual salary of $7,145 automatically rose to $7,775 in July 1964.

John entered teaching after a brief detour that followed his release in January 1958 from a five-year tour of active duty in the Air Force. He worked nine months for IBM, and then as a housing assistant for the New York City Housing Authority before getting his first teaching job and beginning graduate work at Columbia University. He has already earned his M.A.

At Ettinger Junior High, his French specialty places him in a desirable position. The school's students range from the delinquent and the retarded to those at the threshold of learning. Since French is limited to above-average students, John escapes many unteachables, but not in teaching English or remedial reading to other classes that fill out his program.

John moves easily in both worlds — of the teachers and of the pupils. The teaching staff is harmoniously integrated, while as a Negro he has a passport to acceptance by the pupils. Their parents, who readily acknowledge the passport, sometimes take him aside and say, "Whatever you do is all right with me." John insists that the students study, including regular homework, special assignments and projects. He tries to foster habits of independent study. He feels the student must face the odds against them realistically. The inbred, self-centered life of their ghetto tends to distract them from what they are up against. "I believe in shattering their unreal self-image and in building it in more realistic terms," he said. "And for the most part, they accept it from me."

John's point of view extends beyond color, for he is educated, middle class, and committed to teaching. This determines his approach and also influences student reactions, for they sense class differences as well as color among their teachers: "There are Negro children in my school who have a chip on their shoulders, even in confronting me, because of differences in education, background, environment. I have a different outlook.

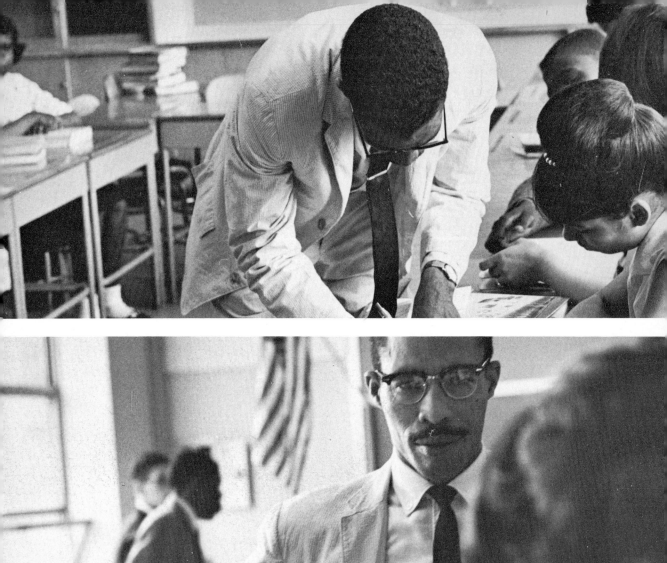

"I speak to them as though they have a lot to gain as individuals, but not as Negro children or as Puerto Rican children. The children react very poorly to this. They say: 'Well, maybe he's being a snob. Who does he think he is? Does he think he is right?'

"The standards that they'll have to confront sooner or later very often are unknown to them. It's a shock, for example, to find out that they will have to be as good and better in the cold practicalities of life than those outside their area. To compete for the same jobs, or for the same scholarships, they'll have to be better because they have one or two strikes against them—coming from a poor neighborhood, coming from a foreign-born family, coming from an immigrant family, coming from a Negro family, or what have you.

"They are prejudiced in their own way. They have their own code and their own way of life, their own philosophy, defective as it may be. To change this, you have to side with them, not verbally, but in attitude. This is what they are more perceptive about. It is not so much what you say as what you are."

At home, Audrey Creary reached lunchtime with three children in tow and three still in school. From ten to twelve o'clock, four-year-old Eve attended a preschool program held in a Parks Department building across Seventh Avenue, near the Harlem River Drive. Carrying baby Rose, Audrey had brought Eve to the pre-school program, walking past eight asphalt tennis courts sandwiched between the subway yards and the low-income Harlem River Houses.

Eve's preschool group of nine boys and seven girls was supervised by a good-natured Parks Department employee who conducts indoor activities in a small but adequate room equipped with standard paint and play facilities. Eve, a vigorous splatterer (her favorite colors are red and green), has four of her paintings and three of her crayon drawings hanging in the Creary dining room. Plump, mature for her age and impish, she overwhelms her baby sister Rose with affection, constantly picking her up and kissing her. Eve is a sunny child.

Martin finished kindergarten at eleven-thirty and ate under the city's free-lunch program, which has been extended to his parochial school. Audrey picked him up at school, although he could walk to his corner without crossing any street. Audrey could watch from the window and direct him across the street. In going to pick him up, Audrey walked through the vestibule of the Church of the Resurrection. The church itself is locked during the day as is common among Harlem's 241 churches. It is an unpleasant reality that Harlem residents take for granted. Not only have Resurrection's poorboxes been pilfered in the past, but even its altar has been desecrated.

Martin left school clutching a prettily pious "pre-primary magazine" that lands in Harlem with a thud, depicting Christianity as an homogenized product of suburbia where parents and pupils, even Jesus and Mary, look as if they come from Shaker Heights or Scarsdale. "You'd think that all children owned cocker spaniels and lived in homes with yards," Audrey commented. She has been a public schoolteacher in Harlem and is familiar with the lot of Negro pupils: "In their situation, of course they're at a disadvantage. The teachers have to dig back, dig down, and try to augment the experiences that are lacking. For example, the children always see the same situation, the same city streets, the same concrete, the same buildings; their experiences are limited."

Carrying Rose and flanked by Martin, Audrey picked up Eve at the preschool class. As they walked home, Audrey looked like a teen-aged babysitter. Trim, buoyant, with a high-pitched voice that goes higher when she is stressing a point, Audrey variously looks like Plain Jane, big sister, teacher, or fashionable suburbanite. John enjoys the fact that his wife at thirty-four attracts whistles from teen-agers. But she can also look like a tired librarian when her glasses slip down her nose. At such times, John makes a point of nudging her glasses back in place. Audrey is considering contact lenses, but the dentist comes first for the extensive care she needs.

In the school library, John joined his usual lunch companions, who include three women members of the Jewish Teachers Association. He is fond of remarking that he is an honorary member of their association and that he integrates it. In effect, he underlines his rejection of the anti-Semitism that persists in Harlem. He also shares the middle-class attitude in American large cities where everyone is conscious of race and religion without, for the most part, discriminating. Munching sandwiches and drinking Sucaryl-sweetened tea, John and his fellow teachers huddled in their oasis in the school library, resting from their strenuous journey through a schoolday in East Harlem.

Since it was the first of the month and therefore payday, John asked, "Are the eagles flying yet?" and was told that the messenger had just left to pick up the paychecks. This prompted a bitter observation by a woman teacher about a poster recruiting subway policemen. The starting salary, with only a high-school diploma, was higher than that of a teacher with a college degree. This touched a sore spot reminding them that education was not getting its just rewards. Next came remonstrations against the Board of Education, clearly a fumbling, indifferent leviathan in the teachers' view. A young teacher was advised when writing about a raise already seven months overdue: "Always keep a carbon and always send your letter by registered mail, return receipt requested, when you write to the Board of Education."

When the teachers talked about the students, it was obvious that—from their middle-class perch—they have as much trouble identifying with the students as the students have in identifying with them. The teachers were exercised over chronic late-comers and found it hard to understand why they couldn't arrive on time. John could have pictured the suffocating home conditions that he had observed when he worked for the Housing Authority — and the familiar problems of broken homes, crowded conditions, and family despair in Harlem. But he listened and said little. His colleagues were obviously not receptive at the time to such explanations, and John realized—probably unconsciously—that it would have done more harm to try to stem the tide of indignation.

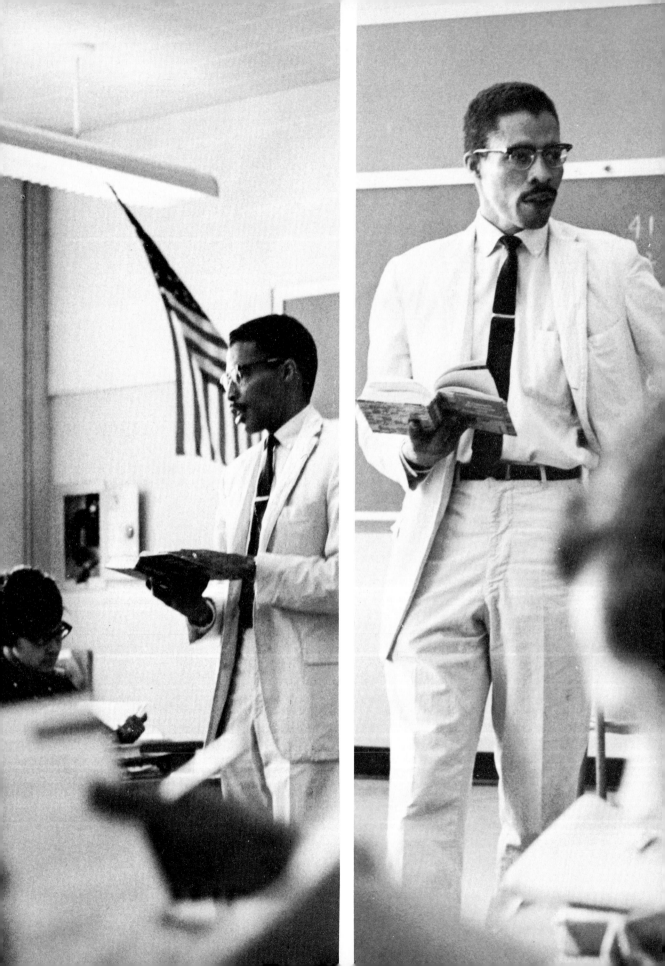

They also talked of the conspicuous and wasteful spending habits of the students. A woman teacher told of meeting a rain-soaked pupil en route to school on the previous morning. She asked him why he didn't have an umbrella. Didn't he get an allowance from which he could save enough to buy an umbrella? When she reported his weekly allowance in dollars—"four"—her voice was filled with outrage that jangled the women teachers' teacups. Another teacher added his illustration: a boy who explained why he couldn't afford a notebook by holding up a cleaning bill for $3.50. There were other comments about the hopeless educational condition in which many pupils arrived at junior high school hardly able to read and write, and unable to follow simple directions. For some teachers, it means facing class after class for which no teachers college has ever prepared them. Confronted with an alien environment and numbers of unteachable pupils, surrounded by a society that undervalues the schoolteacher, and feeling deserted by a coolly distant Board of Education, a white teacher's lot is not an easy one at Ettinger Junior High. But unlike John Creary, he leaves the ghetto when he goes home.

Back in his classroom after lunch, John quizzed a ninth-grade French class, followed by an eighth-grade English class, and a final unassigned period in which he picked up his monthly paycheck. At Dunbar Apartments, Audrey coped with baby Rose, Eve, and Martin, and did some local shopping. At her school, Marianne faced lessons in geography, history, and spelling, and then waited for her father. On the way to pick up Marianne, John usually drops off a fellow teacher who lives in the Bronx. A sympathetic, middle-aged mother who has raised a family while teaching school, she enjoys talking religion with John. On that Friday, as usual, John drove with Marianne to Yonkers and she waited as he gave a private French lesson to a high-school student. This earns an additional twenty-four dollars a month, largely offsetting Marianne's monthly tuition of thirty-five dollars.

The trip home superimposes two contrasting worlds—the Bronx and Yonkers of private homes on tree-lined streets and Harlem. John watches Marianne absorb the contrast. "Every time she comes across the bridge from the Bronx into Harlem, she sees and feels the difference. I can tell from the pensive expression on her face. There's that invisible wall as soon as you cross the Macombs Dam Bridge from the Bronx. There's a difference in the way people walk, the way streets look. The compacting of so many bodies and cars and houses—there's no feeling of freedom, space, movement.

"Marianne doesn't talk a great deal about it, but it comes out in specific things she notices: 'Gee, look at all the children on the street. . . . There's so much traffic. . . . That tree is bent over.' She misses the trees in particular. There are relatively few trees in Harlem when you consider it, and those you almost don't see. Everything else seems to make them disappear. The trees in the middle of Seventh Avenue are not like trees. They are some sort of ornaments."

On these trips to and from the Bronx, the influence of father on daughter is reenforced. It is a time for a child's questions and a father's answers, for a strengthening of Marianne's attitudes, values, and motivation. On the other four weekdays, they return directly to their Harlem home so John can eat an early supper before going to Columbia University's Teachers College where he attended classes from five to seven, Monday through Thursday. With GI Bill aid, John is completing a doctorate in education, with teaching of French as his area of specialization.

On the day before, for instance, John attended a course on "Curriculum in Secondary Education." At Teachers College, as he strode briskly through the main entrance on 120th Street, he assumed his most self-assured role. His mustache, double-breasted raincoat, briefcase, and confident stride recalled the fact that he was an officer in the Air Force. But instead of a briefing, he was going to a seminar discussion on school administration and curriculum changes.

He had gotten up at 3:30 A.M. on that Thursday in order to complete an assignment for the class. After splashing water on his face, he worked until 7 A.M., and left the house at his usual time of seven-thirty. It was one of many indications that John resembles the stereotyped New England Puritan—hard-working, ambitious, early-rising and God-fearing. It also reflects the influence of his father, who had wanted him to attend Harvard and become a doctor. John, who had once wanted to become a Jesuit priest, went to Fordham College and lived at the house of a widower friend of his father's. "I was on my own. I was stubborn, even proud, and I wanted to make my own decisions. Looking back on it now, I was so much like my father, imitating his drive, his determination. The only way to be what you want to be is to do what you should do. We learn by doing and we become by doing. The only way to accomplish something is to work at it. There's always a creative side to work, to see the work of your hands. 'Do thou, O Lord, direct the work of our hands.' "

John's father, a Jamaican who migrated in the mid-1920's, met a Jamaican in New York City and married her in Montclair, New Jersey, in an Italian parish church. John's mother went home for his birth on October 28, 1927, but she wouldn't return to the United States. She refused to accept the Negro's lot in white America.

"My mother's father had been a small landholder just outside of Kingston, Jamaica, and was a tradesman, a shoemaker. On both sides, my parents were of some independent means. My father brought me to this country when I was a year and eleven months, as I remember him telling the story. He was both mother and father to me, and he was going to college, too.

"He dropped out of school somewhere about his senior year, at the height of the depression. He worked as a gardener in Montclair, New Jersey. At the outbreak of the Second World War, since my father was

a very patriotic British subject—as he said —he returned to Jamaica. I was sent to the Jesuit high school in Kingston, and boarded out with a family. I graduated with ambitions of becoming a Jesuit.

"My father didn't like the idea because he felt that my talents were more in the medical line. Well, we had a standoff on that. I graduated at sixteen and went to work as a posting clerk for the government savings bank. Then I taught at my old high school until July 1946, when I returned to the United States, and, in September, I enrolled at Fordham."

John chose to become an American citizen, although his father couldn't understand how he could give up his British passport for the uncertain status of a Negro in America. John holds to a simple explanation. "My roots are here and I owe my loyalty to America." However, even among Negroes in the United States, Jamaicans form a minority within a minority. As Jews are conscious of the Sephardic among them, Italians of Northerners and Sicilians, Irish of Orangemen, the Harlem Negro is conscious of the West Indian. In the easy traffic of ethnic labels, Jamaicans are sometimes called the Jews of Harlem because they succeed in business. They are regarded as the people who work and study hard, save their money, and watch their chances. Coming from a multiracial island, where skin color did not leave deep scars, they pursued the American dream as soon as they landed. For their numbers in Harlem, the Jamaicans always have had a disproportionate share of political power, money, influence, and success. Audrey recalls that she immediately recognized John as a West Indian from his self-confident attitude, his features, and his way of speaking.

Audrey's own background was circumscribed by the American Negro experience. Her parents represent the minority of Negroes in the older generation who made headway against cruel odds. They urged her "to get out," to climb the wall surrounding Harlem — advice that became ironic when she came home again. "My parents had an attitude of superiority. My mother always had the idea that we were a little better than most. She came from a middle-income family and my father worked for the post office. My father is sort of a self-made man and the kind of man who was determined to get where he wanted to be. He's pretty proud of himself."

Audrey's father, originally from Baltimore, moved to New York with his parents as a young man and met Audrey's mother. Her family was from Philadelphia and Atlantic City, but she was staying in New York. Soon after he went to work for the post office, they married. Once Audrey asked about their honeymoon: "My mother said that they took a subway ride and that was her honeymoon. That was all they could afford." Now that her father is retired, her parents live in one of Harlem's luxury apartment houses.

"My father spent thirty-three years in the post office. When he retired, he was a supervisor. My mother was a milliner by trade. She worked in a factory until I came into the world. It was six years after they got married. They thought they weren't going to have any children. And two and a half years later, I had a brother who's now a plumber."

Whereas John took it for granted that he did not belong in a ghetto, Audrey developed this attitude, with considerable help from her parents. Inevitably, their psychological freedom from the ghetto will be followed by physical escape. In this way, the community of Negroes within Harlem or other ghettos is penalized—in the end—by the progress of Negroes.

On Friday evening, as the pace of the week subsides, the eight Crearys have family dinner together and the atmosphere of their personal relations becomes apparent. It is not a matriarchal household. The stereotyped mother-centered Negro household is a lower-class phenomenon; the rising Negro middle-class family, in which the father is the provider with a regular and respectable job, places the authority in the man's hands. The mother may regain much of this authority by default in a move to the suburbs, but the new Negro is less and less a crushed man inside as well as outside the home.

As Harlem child, mother, and teacher, Audrey has watched beleaguered Negro family life. "I remember when I was in school most of the children in my class had keys around their necks. I was one of the very few who came home and my mother would be there. I remember sometimes wishing that I had that independence, going and coming as they did with the keys around their necks and feeling very important. However, if my mother was not there when I got home, I would just feel lost. The child without a mother at home feels the impact. There's something missing.

"I tried working myself a couple of years ago—we had some financial difficulty —and instead of solving the financial problem we only found more problems. It just was complete bedlam and I learned to appreciate my home and my children a whole lot more. So, no matter what happens, I'm determined not to go to work until the children are old enough to stay on their own feet."

In dealing with the children, Audrey is more permissive than John; when he is home, the discipline is firm, even authoritarian. Audrey remarked that she never had any trouble as a Harlem teacher controlling a classroom of difficult children, but "my own children are another matter." Given John's personality and Jamaican background, it is not surprising that he is a dominating head of the household who does not hesitate to discipline the children. While Kenneth has developed his father's penchant for neatness and order, Martin still scatters his clothes to the four corners of the house. The girls are given a freer rein because John feels boys need firm discipline. Marianne, already becoming a second mother around the house, takes her position as the oldest seriously, while Eve still protests, "I want my mommy to put me to bed."

Normally, the family eats Friday dinner at six o'clock, except when friends come for dinner, as they did this Friday. Besides myself, there were Harold and Eleanor, a Negro couple, who arrived as the children's hour was at its peak. Martin was lying in bed forlorn and upset about what had happened on his trip to the store. He had placed a bag of groceries on the ground as he stared at toys in a store window and, when he turned to go home, the bag was gone. The other children played in the bedroom, although Eve and, particularly, Rose wandered in and out of the dining room as John served brandy to the guests. Audrey emerged sporadically from the kitchen to join the conversation, which ranged over the problems of rearing children, of discipline in the schools, of Harold's experiences in boys' work, and John's in the classroom. Eleanor soon joined Audrey in the kitchen to help with dinner.

The friendship between John and Eleanor extends back to college days when both were active at Friendship House, a pioneering interracial center in Harlem that has since closed down. From their manner toward one another and from their reminiscences, it was obvious that two strong personalities had come together, occasionally collided, and emerged friends. John also met Audrey at Friendship House, in the late spring of 1952, when he was a senior at Fordham College in the Bronx and she was a senior at suburban New Rochelle College. Each was a rare Negro student in a white campus community. At first, John was not particularly aware of Audrey at Friendship House: "I don't remember the first time that I met her there, frankly—she didn't impress me at all. It was really afterward that I became aware of her. A whole group of us went up to Pelham to swim. We were playing tag, believe it or not—you know, people twenty-three to twenty-four years of age running around like kids. I happened to have been 'it', and she was the nearest person. She ran like a rabbit. And that was about it." Audrey's version: "I didn't like him at first. I thought he talked too much. But he kept calling me on the telephone, so to put him off I said, 'Okay, I'll go out with you!'"

About six months later, John recalled, they were sitting on a park bench near the Dunbar Apartments. "I said that if we were going to see much more of each other, I'll have to propose so I might as well propose now—'Will you marry me?' And she didn't say 'No.' I was surprised. We were married on August 8, 1953."

In the tandem retelling of their court-ship, with one talking and the other listen-ing, laughing, and interrupting, John and Audrey exemplified how much at ease they are with each other. Besides the romance in their relationship, they obviously like each other very much; hostility from the outside world undoubtedly strengthens this bond. John takes the lead in conversation for he is naturally a talker while Audrey is more of a listener. Although Audrey avoids blunt-ly contradicting what John says, she never hesitates to differ. That evening, Audrey confirmed or disagreed, or, more usually, augmented John's remarks as the con-versation moved inexorably into the Negro problem.

By then the guests were seated at the table for dinner. Eve and Rose as well as John and Audrey ate with the company; the other children had dinner in the boys' room. The conversation became so animated that when the children's bedtime arrived, at eight, the company was still at the table. The children came in to kiss everyone good night or shake hands. Only baby Rose, the family's erratic sleeper, stayed up.

The conversation roamed over the in-evitable topic. Harold and Eleanor, in par-ticular, were addressing a message to me as the white outsider: Negroes resent being tolerated. John explained that "toleration" is a repugnant word in Harlem, since it im-plies condescension. (In another context, a neighborhood cleric cited the outcome of a harmonious social evening involving his Harlem group and a visiting group of white teen-agers. In a post-mortem discussion a Harlem teen-ager expressed the consensus with this reservation: "But they want to help us!") At one point, Harold burst in: "You have no idea of the bitterness among the more successful Negroes. They are the most bitter because they have made it and still are below the white people in their field." Eleanor was still blunter: "The Negro is sick and tired of receiving favors from the white man. And he's still suspicious be-cause he's been burnt so often."

These are increasingly familiar remarks, but they struck like lightning when I heard them in the friendly intimacy of a dining room inside the Harlem ghetto. Although the problem is sociological and national, its context becomes social and personal. The victims of bigotry were sitting across the table, breaking bread with me. They could no more resist poking at the wound of color than a little boy could with a scab on his knee. Negroes seldom have the opportunity to discuss the race problem with white Americans and, on that evening, I was there to listen. For practically all Negroes, it is a frustrating dialogue with the deaf, a reminder of the apartness imposed upon them.

Coffee was served in the living room as the conversation broke into scattered fragments, sometimes involving all at once, sometimes only two at a time. Baby Rose was still lurching about, being picked up, kissed, and put down. It had been a lively and long exchange, but it was time to go home. I drove Harold and Eleanor to their apartment just south of 125th Street.

At the Creary apartment, John moved Marianne and Eve from the bedroom to the living-room couch and put out the lights. It was nearly midnight as John and Audrey got ready for bed. Looking toward the Bronx across Seventh Avenue and the river, some lights were still on. Automobile headlights flashed on Harlem River Drive. On Eighth Avenue, Friday night in Harlem was still young.

When John Creary left his apartment building shortly before eight o'clock on Saturday morning, the insulated quadrangle of the Dunbar Apartments was silent and empty. The buildings are arranged so that tenants enter the interior quadrangle and then walk through an archway into the surrounding streets. It is a brief ritual of passage from a symbolic stockade that is determined to withstand the ravages of Harlem. The Dunbar families are twice surrounded—by the ghetto around them and the city around the ghetto. They are twice removed—from the defeated, the depraved, and the defiled human substrata that they reject and from the white middle-class that hesitates to accept them. In the struggle for respectability and acceptance, the ultimate fighting unit is the family and the struggle is often lonely, always strenuous.

John went out to move his car because of the city's alternate-side-of-the-street parking regulations that clear one side daily in order to sweep the streets. The mechanical sweepers do not appear as regularly as do traffic patrolmen with green fifteen-dollar parking tickets, so John moved his car from the east side of Seventh Avenue. He parked the car in the concrete yard of his parish church on 151st Street, and went for a haircut in the neighborhood, barber shops being one of America's most stubborn strongholds of segregation.

At home, baby Rose, late to bed and late to rise, was still sleeping, but the other five children were building up the disorderly momentum of a day off from school. Audrey fed them breakfast, picked up around the house, and mobilized the children for a family shopping expedition. Before returning home, John went to a check-cashing store on West 145th Street, since the banks were closed by the time he left school on Friday with his monthly paycheck. He paid $2.88 to cash his check for $560.

The haircut and the check cashing were part of John's Harlem life, but Saturday shopping would be outside Harlem. The supermarket chain that the family often patronizes has a branch on 145th Street opposit the check-cashing store, but—as on most Saturdays after payday—the family was going to a spacious, shiny branch in the Bronx. By shopping there, the Crearys turn their back on Harlem. The decision is conscious and purposeful, symbolic and practical, as John explained: "We shop largely in areas that are not segregated. We find that we get better quality food outside Harlem for about the same price. The local supermarkets are not as well kept, not as well stocked with the things that you'd normally be able to buy outside Harlem. For example, we had trouble finding wheat germ or whole grain flour or unbleached rice. It was a long time before we found that outside of Harlem it was relatively easy to come by these things. In the local area, they cater to the limited tastes of the people, if you want to call it that. It's a horrible thing to have to say, but nevertheless true."

As John and Audrey, along with the children, drove north to the Bronx supermarket, they remarked, as on several other occasions, that their first instinct is to get out of Harlem, to leave it behind whenever possible. For the children, such expeditions have the cumulative effect of putting them at ease in the white world, where it is not strange to shop next to a white family or be served by a white clerk. When Audrey was a child, shopping in midtown Manhattan with her mother was a special occasion and it meant getting dressed up.

At the Bronx supermarket, the eight Crearys and their two shopping carts joined the mainstream of American consumers, swept along by the blandishments of the merchandisers' wonderland where shopping is well organized and brightly labeled. The mood was carefree, but the shopping careful. John made a point of looking at price and quantity to confirm that the economy size was actually cheaper, and he avoided brand names in favor of the cheaper equivalents with the supermarket's own label. He takes pride in his prudent shopping, which reflects his meticulous attitude. Audrey picked out food items listed by the weekly New York City market report as abundant and therefore cheaper.

When the Crearys met another Harlem couple, they compared notes on why they were there. They agreed that the Bronx supermarket was cleaner, more pleasant. It had more variety. The service was faster and more courteous. The contrast with the branch on West 145th Street (which I visited later that day) was striking. In Harlem, although practically the same items were available, the merchandisers seemed to be saying: Take it or leave it. The store was drab, the lines long, the clerks indifferent, the shoppers all Negroes; however, in a cursory comparison of prices, no glaring differences were evident.

The psychological reasons for shopping in the Bronx were unmistakable. The Crearys refused to accept confinement to the ghetto. They also were suspicious of Harlem commodities, as if the ghetto even tainted what was sold there. John claimed that some items, such as bread, were slightly stale in Harlem, but that he has confidence in quality and freshness outside Harlem. On weekday afternoons, he does incidental buying in the Bronx as he drives home with Marianne. Clothes and household furnishings are usually bought by Audrey or by both of them; the Sears, Roebuck store in the Bronx and the Cross County Shopping Center in Westchester are favored for such shopping.

On that Saturday, nine bags of groceries costing $42.19, basic supplies for about ten days, were loaded into the station wagon, then unloaded and carried up four flights to the apartment. The rest of Saturday was spent at home; it was an unpleasant fall day, rainy, chilly, and gray. As John looked out the window, he rubbed his finger along the sill. "There's a tremendous amount of soot and it filters right into the house. You'll find a lot of soft coal being used in this area. We're right near the Harlem River, and when the humidity is right, when the ceiling is low in the cold months, you get all the fumes from the soft coal that's stoked up in the early mornings. And, as you can see, there's a lot of traffic that goes by."

During warm weather, the Crearys often go on picnics to Van Cortlandt Park; in the summer, they go swimming at state parks in Westchester and Orange counties. The pattern remains consistent: the family functions as a unit and it escapes from Harlem. The Crearys keep their children away from neighborhood playgrounds when they are not properly supervised. A playground in the center of the Dunbar quadrangle is their favorite play area, although it has been closed on Saturdays because no supervisor is available. As a result, this Saturday the Creary children played on the Dunbar walks, coming in and out of the apartment constantly, punctuating the afternoon by repeatedly ringing the downstairs bell. Marianne, who was complaining that she had nothing to do, received a phone call from a Dunbar playmate and they both went swimming at the Y on 135th Street. Before Marianne left, John reminded her not to show off, to be careful, and to practice her swimming kick.

John watched an Air Force football game on television in the dining room, focal point of the Creary home. Besides the TV set and the dining room table, it contains Marianne's record player, John's tape recorder, his books, and his music records. A bookcase holds all of John's and Audrey's college notes plus their yearbooks. They both retain strong loyalties to the colleges where they felt accepted in a white environment. John's 1952 Fordham yearbook lists his varied undergraduate activities by college years: Sodality, 1, 2, 3; Track, 1, 2, 3, 4; International Club, 4; French Club, 1, 2, 3, 4; Beethoven Society, 2, 3. He received a B.A. degree in French. Audrey, whose maiden name was Roberts, is described in the College of New Rochelle's 1952 yearbook: "We will remember Audrey's love of music, her contralto voice and bursts of song. We will remember, too, that while her major field of concentration is mathematics, her major field of interest will always be people. Tutoring, Girl Scouting, camp counseling, playground work—all these and more reveal a dedicated spirit."

One handwritten salutation filled with collegiate melodrama reflects the acceptance Audrey apparently achieved — and raises the question of what happens to Negro-white friendships after graduation: "May our friendship always be as tremendous as your appetite and that's saying a mouthful.

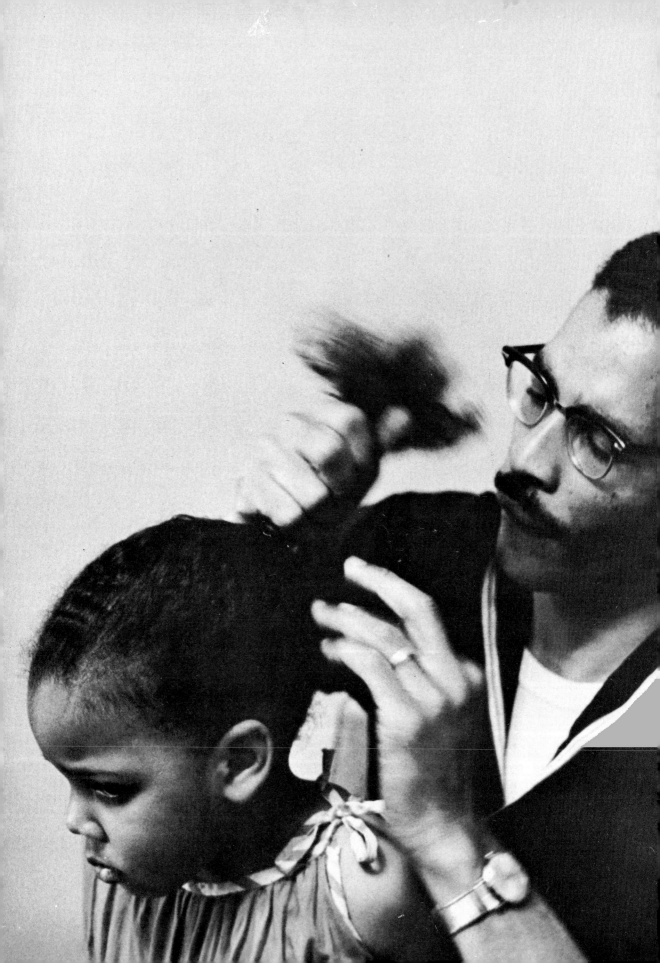

Sincerely tho—now that four years are over —the good old college days are gone, but here's hoping our friendship goes on and on and on." The friendship has gone on, as have others with several former classmates, including Frances, who was to visit that evening with her husband. Although many avoided friendship in the first place, Audrey does not feel deserted by her college friends.

On that Saturday afternoon, as he rooted for the Air Force football team, John pieced together his military experiences. It was a story of acceptance within the confined framework of the Air Force and of shock for Audrey as a northern Negro confronting the South for the first time.

When John enlisted in the Air Force in January 1953, the recruiting sergeant, after looking at his papers, said bluntly: "You've got three strikes against you. You are foreign-born, a Negro, and a Catholic." After John completed his training and was assigned to Florida, Audrey joined him. "The first feeling I had on my way South was amazement. I was just overwhelmed. I'd heard of separate drinking fountains, but I didn't believe it until I saw it. The fact that somebody would ask me to move to the back of the bus . . . I just stopped riding buses from then on . . . Two drinking fountains side by side, one white, one colored . . . As one girl said, she never drank colored water before, so why should she start in now. It was just overwhelming." For Audrey, conditioned to the indirect prejudice of the North, the experience required a complete personal reorientation. For both of them, life became centered on the military base where color was no problem. Only in the North can the Crearys live in the ghetto and walk a shaky bridge into the white world.

Audrey recalled the summer of 1962, when they drove to Florida to visit friends. "Just going down there gets you annoyed all over again." Audrey, who was pregnant at the time, used gas station rest rooms without any trouble until they reached northern Florida. Then the slight indignity that is always around the corner unnerved her. John, in his fashion, remained philosophical. They had stopped for gas, and when Audrey went to use the rest room the attendant said she would have to use "the other one."

"I got annoyed, and though ordinarily I wouldn't have bothered to go in, I did so," Audrey said, her voice rising to a higher pitch. "It was the filthiest place you ever saw. And I came out and said, 'My God, you can treat animals better than that.' I told John that if I had known that, he wouldn't have spent his money there. I was almost in tears, I was so mad. And John said, 'What are you getting so excited for? You've been through this before.' It's just the idea all over again." When they talked about the incident with their Negro friends in Florida, they learned of the standard driving technique in the South: You don't buy gas if you have to use the "other" rest room. And it works.

Within the Air Force, John's personal weapons—education, energy, determination—were effective. He eventually won a place in officers' candidate school, although he needed friendly intervention when his application became bogged down. He barely made the age requirement. After being commissioned on September 9, 1955, John attended personnel officers' school. When he left active service in January 1958, as a first lieutenant, he had served five years in the Air Force, three of them as an officer in Libya, in Illinois, and at Mitchell Air Force Base (now deactivated) on Long Island. He has since been promoted to captain in the Air Force reserve.

Nonetheless, the civilian problems of housing and of acceptance persisted. When the Air Force did not provide housing, John and Audrey became like any other Negroes. They looked, were rebuffed, and looked again until they found a place. John recalled his experiences in moderate tones: "At Mitchell Air Force Base, we couldn't find anything, despite the fact that there were a number of advertised homes for sale and for rent. We couldn't either rent or buy. This was in 1958 in Nassau-Suffolk County. As a matter of fact, I complained to the base housing officer that specification of the color of applicants for homes should not be on the base bulletin board. It was out of place on a federal reservation and as tactfully as possible, I tried to make a point."

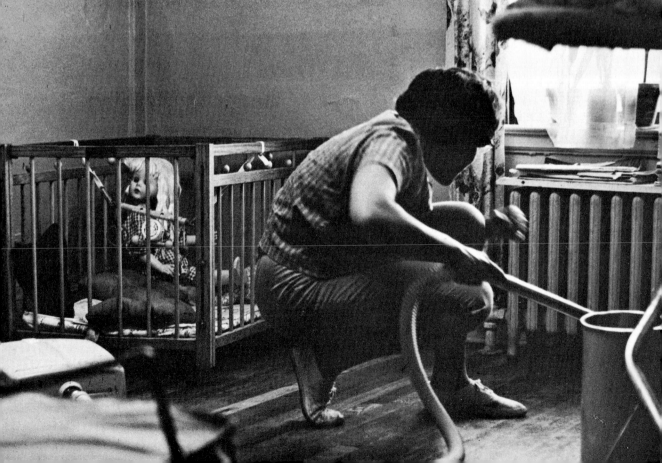

Without flamboyance, John the officer as well as the civilian refused to be treated as a Negro: "You speak as an individual and very often you can be looked at as somebody who's different, not for what you're saying but because of how you seem. The tendency is for people not to consider you as an individual, but merely to stop at the surface. This is one of my biggest gripes. When I go to Reserve meetings I get the feeling that some of my costudents in the seminars wonder how come a Negro speaks the way he does or is doing exactly the same thing—at the same level and, in some cases, beyond."

Neither John nor Audrey wants to be acutely self-conscious of color, and their reactions are not dominated by the fact of color. John, in particular, has developed the ability to stand back and look at the painful consequences of being a Negro. Consequently, the reminiscences of prejudice in their Harlem dining room—as the TV blared, the doorbell rang, the children shouted—were abstracted, with personal bitterness removed. Like other educated middle-class Negroes, the Crearys can sound like well-informed victims of an illness who have read up on the symptoms, the treatment, and the possibilities of a cure. They almost sound as if it didn't hurt at all.

As Saturday afternoon dissolved in desultory conversations and cups of coffee, the televised football game received intermittent attention. Audrey did some housework, John smoked filter-tip cigarettes, and baby Rose wandered in and out of the dining room sucking her thumb. Audrey, in one of those irrelevant observations that a mother makes, noted that her second, fourth, and sixth children have been thumb suckers. All six have been nursed by their mother. As John lifted Kenneth and Joseph so they could chin themselves on the doorway, he talked of his concern for their physical fitness. John himself was a dash and relay track man in college, Audrey an accomplished swimmer.

There was other incidental intelligence. John goes off alone to a double-feature movie when he feels tense and moody. Audrey recognizes the mood when he complains that the house is a mess. Audrey finds knitting relaxing—when she has time for it. Television is strictly rationed for the children, limited almost exclusively to morning viewing.

It was now dark outside, and all the children were home. They ate supper, played awhile, and then were hustled off to bed. Company was coming soon. John put on a clean white shirt and a bow tie. Audrey, finally freed of her household chores, changed into a frilly green blouse and grey skirt. Scotch was on the table, ice in a bowl, the lights were dimmed, and the transition completed from the children's hour to company time.

As two white couples arrived (a Negro couple was unable to come at the last minute) and drinks were poured, the apartment seemed adrift on its own island. There was no Harlem, no ghetto, just conversation and friends. The race problem didn't exist. John and Audrey, host and hostess, did not have to act as social intermediaries in the kind of interracial situation where both sides feint, circle, and sniff socially. Audrey's former classmate, Frances, and her lawyer-husband had driven from Westchester, while Bill, John's fellow teacher at his East Harlem high school, had come with his wife by subway from the Bronx. The social group had come together the way any other might have—through school and job. The compatible classmate or colleague had become the friend invited for drinks. Negro and white had not come together to demonstrate racial harmony. Some friends had dropped over.

Late in the evening, the visiting wives went into the living room to look at recent Creary family pictures. And, in the dining room, the husbands were heatedly discussing the legal profession (there was a lawyer present) and education (there were two teachers present). When Audrey went to the kitchen to prepare an after-midnight buffet, the two white housewives willingly talked about their racial attitudes. The race problem is too thoroughly explored and reported to expect new insights from the two white couples on how they came to regard the Crearys as friends like any others. While their viewpoints were not identical, they regarded their friendship with the Crearys as a natural result of contact and compatibility.

The women spoke with feeling as mothers who want their children to enjoy the advantages of mixed friendships in a mixed America. They didn't want their children to live sheltered lives in which they met only their own kind, either racially or religiously. Whereas the Crearys, as parents living in Harlem, fear contamination of their children by the sordid in their surroundings, these conscientious mothers reject artificial isolation of their children. Neither wants to live in a ghetto.

Then the snacks were ready, the coffee brewed, and the evening ended as we ate cold cuts, cheese, and rye bread and recalled Audrey's college days. (Frances insisted that Audrey hasn't changed since then.) Soon, both couples went home to relieve their babysitters. The couple from the suburbs drove the couple from the Bronx home from Saturday night in Harlem.

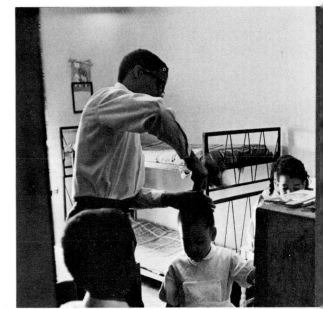
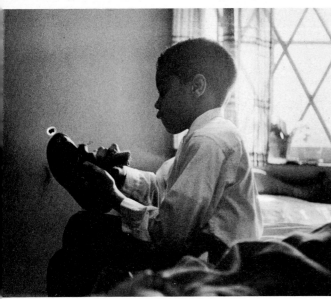

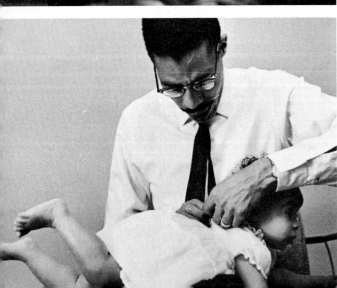

In the Church of the Resurrection on Sunday morning, the radiators hissed in the background as the white priest droned in Latin at the altar in front of the black congregation. The Creary family sat halfway back on the left of the center aisle. John held baby Rose. Marianne sat between Audrey and John, and then, in a row: Martin, Kenneth, Joseph, Eve. When John went to the altar to receive Communion, Eve promptly tagged along.

It was a subdued congregation, each individual pursuing his own path of worship, focused on the Sunday Mass or on private thoughts. As part of a well-organized superstructure, the Catholic parish does not alter its style in Harlem; the sermon topic, the pleas for money, even the announcements of parish meetings resemble counterparts across the Harlem River. But Catholic churches in Harlem lack Negro priests and nuns and so serve religion with a white hand. Besides the Negro nun in the parish school, Resurrection had one young Negro priest of Jamaican parentage. Its pastors have always been white.

Appropriately, the Catholic sermon throughout the New York Archdiocese concerned religious vocations; at Resurrection, it was delivered by a visiting white priest who celebrated the Mass. He was sincere, well intentioned, and uninspiring. Yet, he avoided the possible pitfalls. He was not condescending. He did not berate. He exhorted with dignity. But he did not confront the central social fact in the lives of the congregation — de facto segregation in a black church operated mainly by white priests.

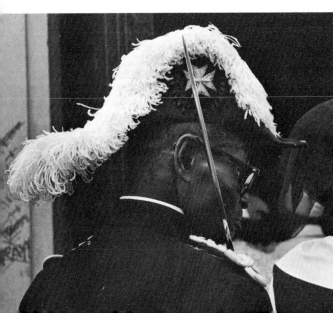

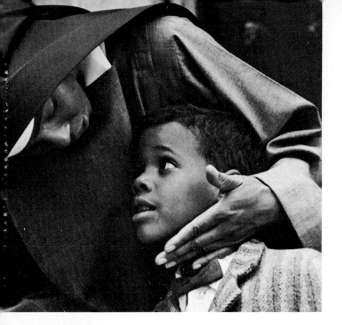

John and Audrey were attentive to the sermon. They had come not to hear a call to arms but, primarily, to attend Mass. While they do not hesitate to criticize sermons or more serious matters such as the bias of committed Christians, the thought of rejecting their religious faith is too far-fetched for them to consider. John is particularly aware of Negro friends who have rejected Christianity because it has not practiced its preaching on the race problem. Instinctively, he feels such Negroes are ordering their lives and their reactions mainly on the basis of color, placing themselves in double jeopardy to the injustice of prejudice. John resents being thought of as a Negro rather than as an individual, and so in refusing to reject Christianity for its failures in the race issue, he is being consistent. John likes to be consistent.

The faith of John and Audrey, with its eye on principles although not blinded to practices, undoubtedly sustains them. It is personal and important, often cropping up in conversation. When asked what supports them in a strenuous struggle with bills, budgets, and bias, and in a family adventure whose outcome will not be clear until the children grow up, they answer, "Our religious faith keeps us going." It is a facile answer but it does seem to touch the roots of their existence.

After the twelve-thirty Mass, the Crearys chatted with friends in the vestibule of the church as their children scattered. Outside, a neighborhood youth, home from Yale for the weekend, talked with Father Dugan, a priest who personifies the white clergyman in Harlem. He came to Resurrection shortly after the war as a young priest and has remained. Father Dugan approaches his work neither as a missionary in Harlem nor as a neutral who ignores the special problems of his parishioners. Although each white clergyman makes his own adjustment to a Harlem assignment, depending on his own make-up, Father Dugan had confirmed at an earlier meeting the common ingredients. Negroes resent condescension and they are alert to the attitude of any white person in their midst, not specifically for what is said, but for what can be sensed. Father Dugan also has a sense of humor and an informal manner. He let Eve hide in his clerical cape as he talked to the Crearys.

On the way home, Audrey and Kenneth stopped at the Greek grocer's on Seventh Avenue to buy Italian salami, ale, and bread; the grocer promised that the black olives that John likes would arrive on Monday. The rest of the family went directly to the apartment for what is a disorganized, stay-at-home day when the weather is not warm enough for outings or not hot enough for swimming. During the summer, the family is likely to cook its Sunday meals outdoors after attending early church, but during the school year, the Crearys often go to church in shifts, with Audrey attending seven A.M. Mass so that she can prepare breakfast for the family. John likes to sleep late and read *The New York Times* in bed. On this Sunday, when the children were watching morning television, a stereotyped Negro cartoon character was portrayed—shiftless, dull witted, obsequious. After switching off the program, Audrey and John each made calls to the station to complain.

During the school year, Sunday afternoon dinner is usually followed by an evening at home, with John supervising and assisting the children with their homework. Then John and Audrey watch television. It is the final familial re-enforcement before the week begins. However, on this particular Sunday the family was to embark on what might be called an adventure in suburbia.

It turned out to be a lesson in patience and prudence, an exercise of good will, a demonstration of a desire for interracial understanding, and also a familiar experience for John and Audrey of being at the brink of rejection. On the other hand, for six suburban New Jersey couples, who were expecting them, it was a painless lesson in race relations, an exercise in sugar-coated courage. It also was a demonstration of how "suburbanitis" can lead to social withdrawal.

The Crearys were invited to meet several couples who belong to a church discussion group. The situation and the community were typical, so names are not significant. It is enough to note that the Crearys were invited by committed Christians, without specifying whether the moderator of the church group was a priest or minister. Call him Pastor George and place the Crearys in the midst of three elements: white, Christian, and suburban.

Their invitation was arranged by a resident of the community who had been active in Harlem interracial work. Although the community has its own small ghetto, inviting Negroes from across the river was undoubtedly safer since distance discourages familiarity. At three o'clock, I left Harlem with the Creary family for the home of the intermediary who had invited them to Sunday dinner before the evening meeting. The Creary boys were sprawled in the rear of the station wagon, Eve and Marianne were in the back seat, Audrey held Rose in the front, and John drove. Within an hour, via the George Washington Bridge and Palisades Parkway, we were in the alien territory of well-tended lawns, and prudent property owners. When we arrived, our hostess greeted us enthusiastically. She kissed John and Audrey, introduced her husband and her five children, and made us all feel at home. Apparently, we were being girded with genuine warmth for what lay ahead.

With the arrival of Pastor George after dinner, the amiable chitchat about children, work, and mutual friends was transformed into a pretrial discussion about the meeting at which John and Audrey were to be the Negroes of the night. Pastor George explained that he was under considerable pressure from his parishioners just for prodding them to meet a Negro couple. John and Audrey chatted matter-of-factly with him. They didn't even blink at the mimeographed questions that were to start off the evening. The couple from Harlem were to be asked:

1. *Are there many Negroes in your parish? Do they feel at home there?*
2. *What kind of work do they do? Is race a factor in this field?*
3. *What is your neighborhood like? Are the people happy there?*
4. *Is adequate education available for families such as yours?*

Pastor George, a progressive young prelate who is literal about Christianity, admitted that he was amazed at the antipathy aroused by the proposal that his parishioners meet a Negro couple. His group was divided into small discussion units and half of them had already turned down his proposal. "After all," he said, "is it so much to ask them to love their fellow man?" No one answered. He felt that it was his duty to explain the situation to the Crearys.

Incredibly, John and Audrey retained their composure as they were told, in effect, that they were social lepers. But Pastor George was not to blame; he was going as fast as possible in the face of stubborn escapism. Many parishioners just didn't want to face a Negro couple, much less the Negro problem. That same morning his parishioners had been indignant at the presence of CORE pickets; one of them remarked: "Why did they have to picket in front of the church? They could have picketed in front of the bakery. Everyone goes there after church."

Pastor George described a last-minute tempest that developed when he told the couples that a white friend of the Crearys would observe their gathering. The local pediatrician's wife, at whose newly purchased home the meeting would be held, told the clergyman bluntly, "We don't have a chair for him!" The other couples also made it clear that they would feel uncomfortable with an outsider present, so Pastor George feared that the evening would be a failure if I came along. When he reported that his Christian couples "don't want to be put under a microscope," Audrey lost her composure for the only time that evening. She blurted out, "But we've been under a microscope all our lives!" This settled it; I went along.

We left the Creary children in the care of the friendly housewife who had provided dinner, and departed under Pastor George's escort, clutching mimeographed sheets that would be distributed at the meeting. The six couples were given copies of "The Christian Problem," as the mimeographed statement was titled, and one could hardly ask for a more direct confrontation of Christianity and color:

It is important to recognize first that interracial conflict is much more of a problem for the white Christian than it is a problem for the Negro. The Negro who has been offended by the sin of prejudice can one day look forward to vindication and reward from his Father in heaven. On the other hand, the white man who is guilty of the sin of prejudice will one day stand before God and have to give an account of himself. And to him Our Lord will say, "I was hungry and thirsty and homeless and alone . . . and you ignored me, you rejected me . . . depart from me, you cursed." We were given the name of Christ in Baptism, we call ourselves Christians. If the love of Christ for all others is not in our hearts then this name is a mockery, a perversion. The heart of the problem is the refusal on the part of the white Christian to recognize the Negro as an individual human being, with feelings that can be hurt, with desires that can be frustrated, with the constant vivid realization that the great majority of whites who call themselves Christian are not only indifferent to his needs, but are actually hostile.

The purpose of this meeting is to come together with a fellow Christian, to learn, to gather material for an examination of conscience, to develop a commitment to Christian love, to seek areas of Christian action, which by working to free the Negro from his bonds, we might become more Christlike, to gain for ourselves a greater measure of the freedom of the children of God.

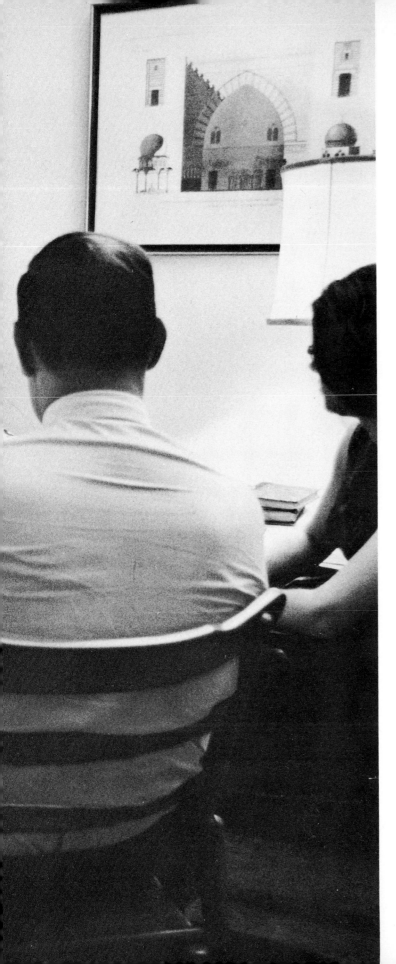

As the evening got under way, with pleasantries and pauses that were quickly and politely filled, it became evident how much Audrey and John resembled the other couples in their social style. Except that they had the advantage of being black and, therefore, of not feeling guilty. Meeting the Crearys seemed like a maximum adventure for these couples, cordial, well meaning, full of intramural jokes and white-collar cordiality. One could only wonder: What generation of young lions is being reared in front of their television sets? And if these were the brave ones who were willing to go only as far as this antiseptic meeting, what manner of reluctant parishioners were home watching the Ed Sullivan show? Audrey and John were affable, dignified, and alert. The confrontation in suburbia was beginning.

For the Crearys, who had recently been guests at a similar meeting in a Bronx neighborhood undergoing integration, the middle-class suburban encounter presented no problems. Because John did most of the talking—elaborating, explaining, and occasionally rambling—he removed any social awkwardness. Listening is painless participation. In the Bronx encounter, the Crearys had faced a group who wanted to know how to facilitate integration, and a few who were openly hostile. But that group was more sophisticated about race problems and was accustomed to speaking out in a city where ethnic awareness is taken for granted.

The first questions from suburbia concerned housing, a pressing concern for these couples who, as their incomes rose, would sell their homes and move. The Crearys were asked, "Why would a Negro want to move into the white sections of our town? Wouldn't he be more comfortable where there are other Negroes?" In other words they were asked: Why doesn't he take his problem elsewhere, especially since it will hurt property values? John explained that he wouldn't move into an area only because the residents were all Negro or all white. He would move because it offered him the housing he wanted for his family. They had addressed the question to him as a Negro and he answered as would a fellow member of the American middle class.

An interlude about the Black Muslims diverted the discussion as all criticized them safely. John, however, inserted the warning that the Muslims feed on the impatience of the Negro, implying but not saying that the impatience was caused by towns such as the one he was visiting.

Inevitably, sex reared its head. The wives, in particular, were concerned about interracial dating and interracial marriage. They expressed concern that children of interracial marriages would become helpless victims of prejudice. John reminded them that prejudice was learned at home and he also mentioned successful interracial marriages among his friends. He could have added that both he and Audrey had dated white friends without awkwardness, and that he personally knows of seventeen successful interracial marriages among his friends, with children doing "better than average" in school, in social adjustment, and in outlook. The couples include six white men and eleven white women, almost all now living in mixed neighborhoods and raising an average of four children per family. It is characteristic of John's encounters with white friends and acquaintances that he doesn't open fire wildly; his words that evening were milder than his attitudes. As far as John and Audrey are concerned, marriage is between human beings, not between colors.

As the evening went on, Audrey added her comments to John's in more personal and direct terms. He generalized, she specified. Meanwhile, surprisingly strong pro-Negro statements were made by the suburbanites. At various times, the need to end job injustice was mentioned. One husband even remarked that he would not object if his daughter married a Negro as long as they were well suited to each other. Color didn't matter. Another denounced his church for not taking positive steps on race relations and dressed down Pastor George for not bluntly refuting parishioners who worried about lower property values if Negroes moved in. He said it wasn't true that property declined in value and said this was borne out by readily available statistics.

John argued against a job quota favoring the Negro as a wrong-headed approach and insisted, instead, on hiring and firing according to ability and seniority—which he noted is not being done. This elicited a stronger statement from one of his listeners, who insisted that a preferential job quota was needed. John conceded that his own view would receive a strong dissent from most Negroes. When pressed for suggestions on what could be done by the group in that living room, John was vague, stressing that individual contacts "such as tonight" would bring about greater understanding.

An intuitive mechanism seemed to be at work. John was reacting—without apparent premeditation—to the social radar of the situation and sending out suitable answers and appropriate comments. If the American middle class harmonizes its social activities by remaining sensitive to the reactions of others—by other-directing itself—the Negro needs even more highly developed antennae. To be reasonable is often more persuasive than to harangue, which embarrasses without influencing and risks hardening attitudes. In handling the situation gently, John was demonstrating his social sensitivity. Coffee, lemon meringue pie, and chocolate cake sweetened and smoothed out the evening.

By the time we left at eleven o'clock, it seemed that the Crearys had met the convinced and the converted; the part of the congregation that needed to hear their message was not present. We were practically certain—until we chatted afterwards in the car that the group was ready to do whatever it could to further race relations with Pastor George. In his straightforward, naive manner, he described what happened when he had proposed to this same group of six couples that each invite a Negro couple to their home for coffee. They had vehemently and indignantly rejected the proposal. They would huddle together and meet *a* Negro couple en masse, these same bold suburban adventurers who wanted to work for integration, who could even say they would let their daughters marry Negroes. But, as it turned out, they weren't even willing to let a Negro visit their homes in full sight of their neighbors.

Their attitude provokes indignation. But indignation oversimplifies what is a complex white attitude toward the Negro—and a highly ambiguous one. The words of the suburban liberal are stronger than his actions, a disheartening fact of life for the Negro who hears one thing and sees another. Negroes have long learned not to jump to conclusions in dealing with whites.

Because John and Audrey can identify with white middle-class counterparts (although the opposite is seldom the case), they can understand white reactions. It helps them to employ the necessary Negro art of self-control. Later John admitted that rage was welling up, but he kept it down "somewhere around chest level." John and Audrey also seem able to tranquilize their own reactions, and have at least partly immunized themselves so that they will not be overwhelmed by bitterness. While perceiving the implications of situations, they do not permit themselves to register all rebuffs emotionally. Weeks later Audrey could recall Pastor George's revealing remark that, of course, the Crearys were not typical Negroes, implying that they were acceptable because they were not like the "rest." She had not missed the implication, but had suppressed her reaction.

Why did John and Audrey visit Pastor George's group in the first place? On the way home, John explained in general philosophical terms that it was important for these people to have direct contact with Negroes; this was a way to help them change. Audrey felt, "It was a chance for me to do something, to be of service. If it weren't civil rights, it would be something else. Otherwise, I am completely taken up with caring for the family." Several days later, John said of the trip: "They were experimenting with us and we were experimenting with them. I was really curious about what makes them tick." John and Audrey had increased their range of contacts with their counterparts in middle-class America, and it was another trip out of Harlem.

When Pastor George brought the Crearys back to the friendly house where they had eaten dinner and where the children were waiting to be taken home, Joseph was sleeping on the couch in the living room and the other five children were playing with toys on the floor. Once in the car, the children resumed their places and were soon asleep. John, despite his pride in being efficient and methodical, got lost on the trip back, reaching the George Washington Bridge after a circuitous detour. They arrived home in Harlem after midnight, feeling neither defeated nor self-righteous, but concerned about the next day, about getting up early the next morning, about school. They did not look back on the evening. Their eyes were on tomorrow.

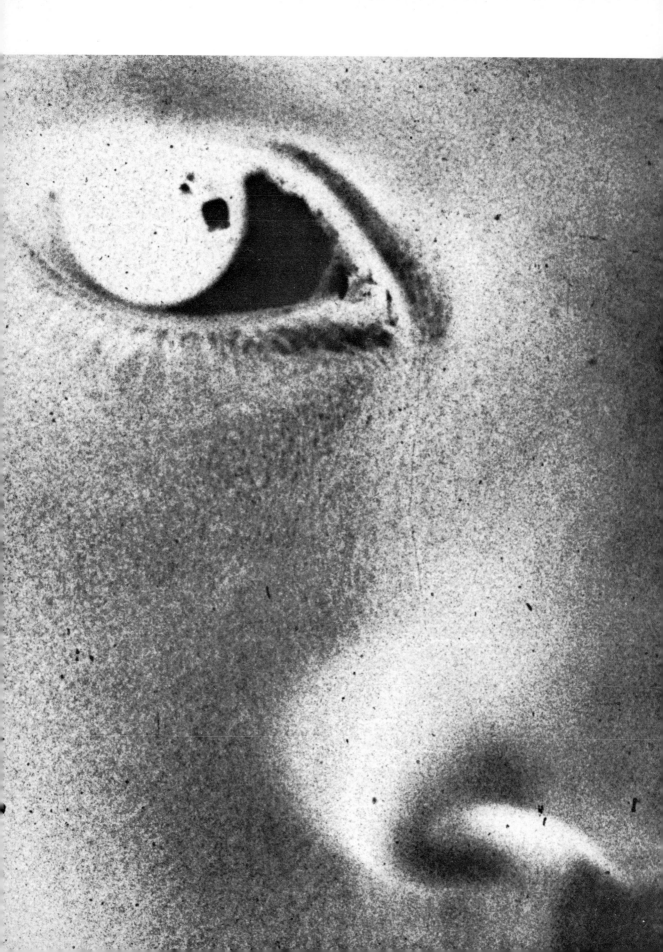

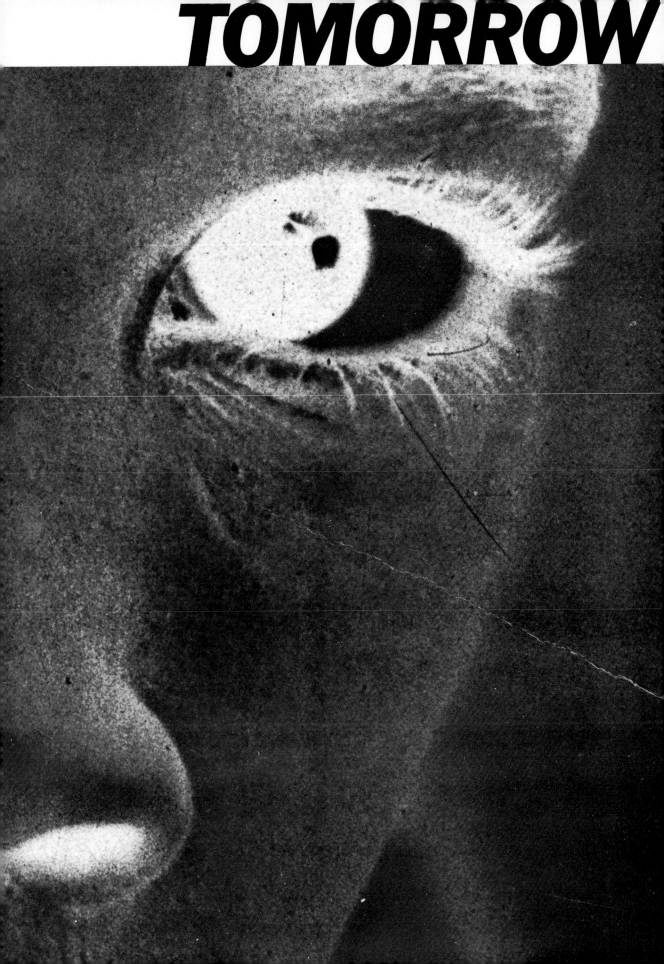

TOMORROW

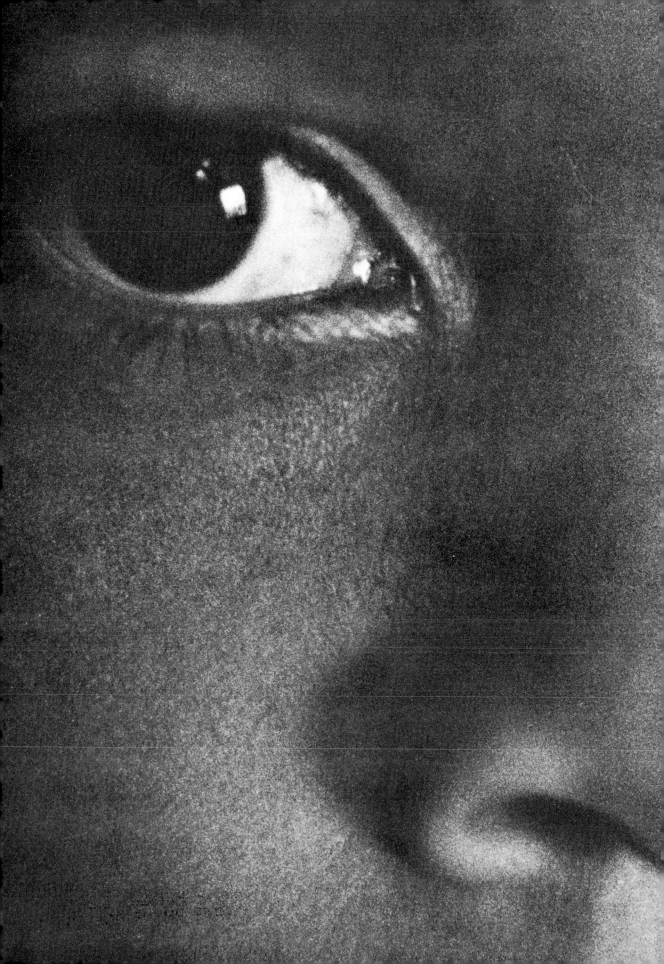

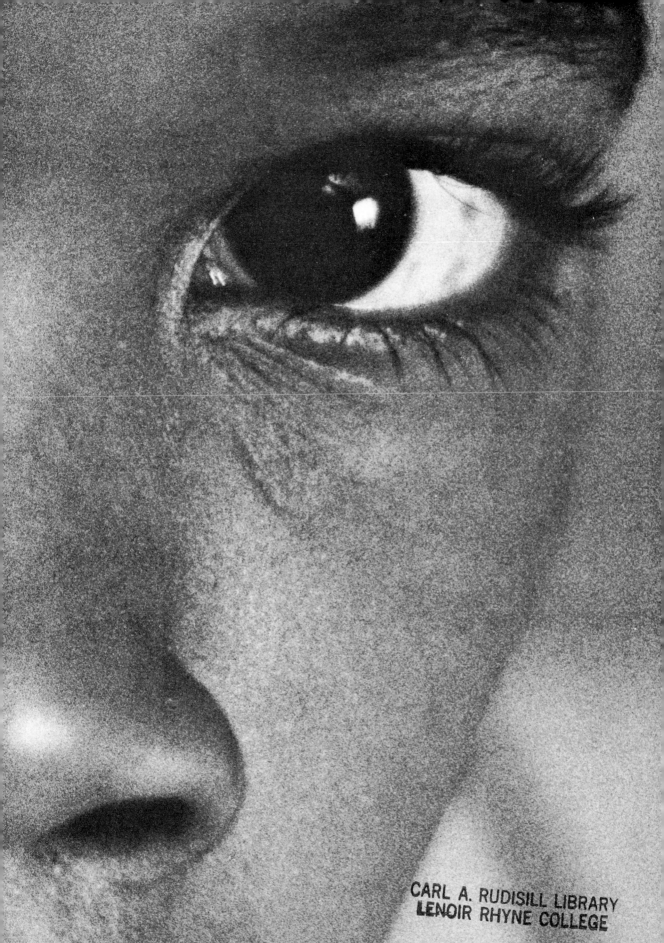

Muhammad Speaks

In Los Angeles:

RIPS 'KKK IN COP CLOTHES!'

Minister Blasts Mayor

The Right Of Self Defense

TO HELP OUR BROTHER
IN BIRMINGHAM ALA
The SPOT LITE BAR
WILL DONATE
ONE DAYS PROFITS
OF WED. JUNE 5th
TO REV. MARTIN LUTHER KING
BACK OUR BROTHERS MOVEMEN

Please BELIEVE THIS
OUR EFFORTS IN BEHALF
OF THIS STRUGGLE IS SINCERE
BECAUSE WE WOULD BE
BITTEN BY DOGS IF WE
WERE IN ALABAMA AND SO
WOULD YOU. IF THIS APPLIES TO YOU
IF WE HAD MORE THAN ONE PLACE
IN TOWN WE WOULD DO THE SAME THING

MADAME DORA
HEALER
&
ADVISOR
UN4-9182
· 260 ·

U.S. POLICY OF DEMOCRACY AND STATE RIGHTS

DOG

BEAST

BARBER

PROCESSING

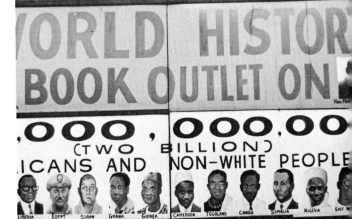

The new generation of Crearys—Marianne, nine; Kenneth, eight; Joseph, six; Martin, five; Eve, four; Rose, one—already are coming into a legacy of escape and acceptance. They are escaping psychologically from the cramped, despairing, introverted world of Harlem and the black ghetto. Benefiting from their parents' social acceptance, they already know a world that is not all black. Sometimes, except for them, it is all white.

While they could become alienated from the Negro world, the Creary children will not feel like strangers in the white world. Not only will they be carried forward by the Negro surge, they will not think like second-class citizens but like middle-class Americans—for better or for worse. While they may not achieve total integration, they will not take for granted the separation between white and Negro. Their legacy from John and Audrey is preparation in attitude and training for membership in the wider social and economic community around them. Insofar as the accelerated acceptance of Negroes permits membership in the society of Americans, the Creary children will be prepared to participate. The invisible wall is tumbling down around them and within their personalities. This is their tomorrow.

Both John and Audrey are optimistic. They realize that they have to be in order to carry on. "We had it easier than our parents and our children will have it easier," Audrey said. "Each generation is better off than the previous one." Their optimism has a guaranteed minimum.

"We hope for a better life for the children and are trying—we hope and plan—to make a better life primarily by education and through the training that we can give them at home," John said. "We are raising them as Catholics, as Christians, as Americans—in the better sense of these terms. We also want them to be realistic—not just idealistic."

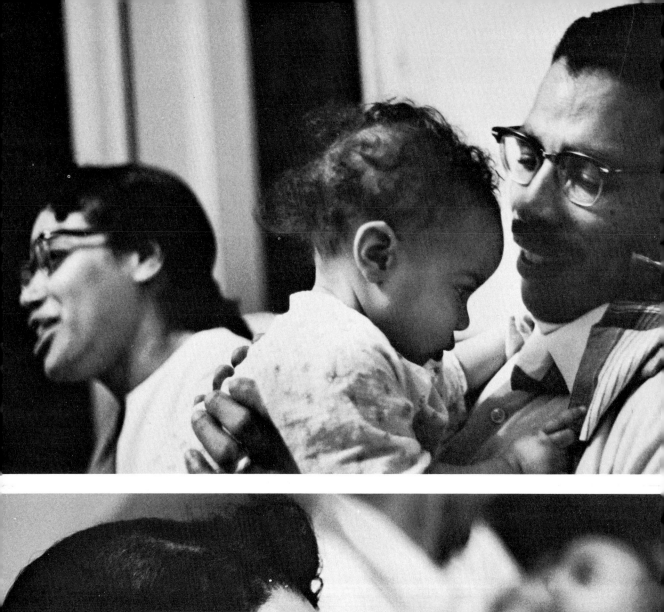

Yet each Creary child must ultimately confront his color alone and within himself. No parent and no preparation can guarantee the outcome of that crucial reaction and its indelible effect on the child as a man or woman. It is the precarious gamble that makes the story of the Creary family—or any Negro family—an adventure with uncertain outcome in a rapidly changing situation. Each of the children must discover his own identity in his personal tomorrow.

Awareness of color undoubtedly comes at an early age. When Audrey taught first-grade pupils in a mixed neighborhood, the children were already noticing which classmates were black, which white, and comparing complexions. John remembers vividly his own childhood experience in the third grade, when he was called "Kid Chocolate" while running in the playground. "All of a sudden there was this difference. I was about seven or eight at that time. I asked, 'What do you mean by that?' And one of my classmates said, 'Nothing, nothing.'

"So it was just dropped at that, though I became aware that there was some difference. And I mentioned the incident to my father, who said: 'Well, you'll just have to accept the fact that you are dark skinned. There's nothing wrong with being dark skinned. People have lighter skins. There's nothing wrong with being lighter skinned.' That was a very simple answer and I was able to accept it. And I think this is the attitude I still have."

Audrey recalls an eighth-grade experience that hints at her own adjustment. She was sent to represent her elementary school at a Police Department program for Negro children. A police inspector, who spoke to the children as a Negro speaking to Negroes, told them, "Once you go out your door after you look in your mirror, you forget that you are a Negro." Audrey says, "After that, now and then I would think back and say to myself that what he said is true. Once you get away, you forget all about it. And most of the time in school that's the way it was. Just another person with the same problems that everybody else had."

With their six children, the Crearys openly confront color variations and comparisons, but try to remove invidious overtones. John is consistent when he harps on the fact that color is accidental: "I could conceive of my child not being considered Negro, considered as a different subdivision of the human race, if that were possible. He might be a Korean or a Japanese. This is my child. He is a person first of all and this is the only thing that really matters. The color of his skin is incidental.

"There is a wide variety of coloration in our family. It is something that distinguishes each child one from the other. There are no two of them alike. They appreciate themselves and their brothers or sisters as they are, as far as we can see. There is nothing defective in Joe being a darker brown, Marianne being a very light tan, Rose being pinkish—God knows what you'd call it—creamy-colored. This is a wonderful thing in its own way. Eve in the summer becomes as brown as a nut and in the winter becomes a very interesting tan. The baby is getting a pointed nose. Joe has a large, flaring set of nostrils—these are the things that make them so different.

"The eyes, they say, are the windows of the soul and in each of these children's eyes there is a depth. Kenny just about drinks you in, he just about drowns you in his eyes. He's a bright, very deep child in so many ways. He's a world all within himself. There are flashes of very, very prankish humor, depths of seriousness, a kind of responsibility. He's a young man to be. He fights. He's got a tremendous will and he's learning how to mold and choose and do the things that are constructive. He's young, he has difficulties, but he's got a tremendous ability to grasp knowledge. It's amazing how he, a child of eight, can pull out the key idea from different but related things. This is a child as he should be.

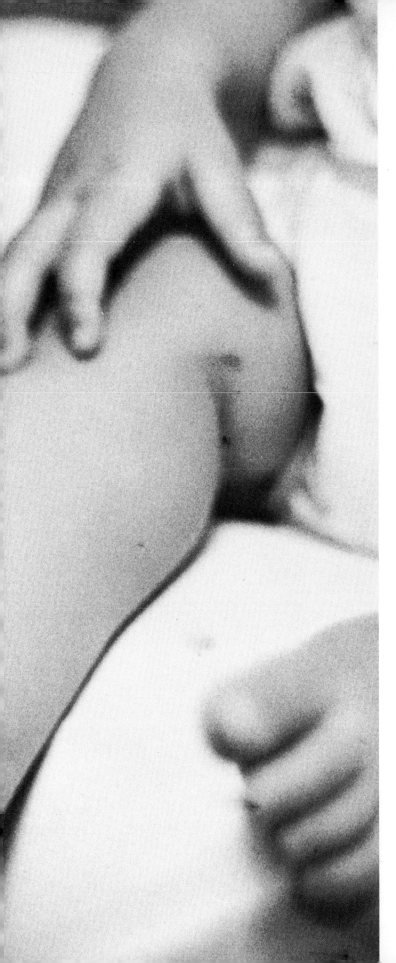

"Take the baby, for example. The baby wants to clap her hands and yet sometimes if she sees me sitting quietly, maybe thinking or doing nothing, and she wants to attract my attention or get everybody's attention, she puts her hands together in an attitude of prayer.

"Praying is something the children do together, Audrey with them. The things that are most significant about the children is that they are taking on our set of values. This is a calculated thing."

In the summertime of bathing suits and beaches, color differences are pronounced. But John is convinced that there is nothing negative about his children's awareness, that there is something positive about it. "Everybody loves that summer tan. It's a kind of a joke, for example, when the bathing suit comes off: 'Gee, he's getting all sorts of checkerboard-type coloration.'

"As far as other people are concerned —to recall a situation during the summer on the beach—Marianne admires the way people who are Caucasian have got a color almost like hers: 'Gee, they can get color almost like mine, but I have a headstart. I've got a better tan than anybody.' Almost in so many words. Or: 'How come I peel and Joe doesn't?' Joe has a much higher pigmentation. Daddy loses skin. Audrey loses practically her whole back. Marianne loses just about as badly as her father. Joe never. Martin seldom. Kenny asks, 'Why does the skin slough off? What happens? Does it really get burned? Why did it get brown? Oh, it's like toast.' Or something like this. This is the kind of analogy they have been able to make."

Still talking in terms that can be meaningful to his children, John added: "Actually, there's nothing wrong with being brown, with being tan. This is the way things are. Leaves change colors. This seems to sum up their attitude. One of the children once brought up the question of what's the matter with people whose skin don't have so much color? Almost as if not to have color is a kind of defect."

Marianne, the oldest of the children, and the first to be sent on her own into a white environment, has been well prepared by her experiences. From the beginning, her godparents were white, her first playmates were white children at the Air Force bases where John was stationed, children who did not show prejudice. Soon after Marianne's transfer from the predominantly Negro neighborhood school to the predominantly white Mt. St. Ursula Academy, she asked her mother, "Am I white?" Audrey answered that Marianne was a mixture, partly white, partly Negro, partly American Indian—a mixture of her mother and father and their mothers and fathers. She told Marianne that "the only thing that you can call yourself is human."

For all the Creary children, the family photo album has implicitly delivered this message as their parents identify the people in the family background. John's paternal grandmother was fair-skinned, blue-eyed, brown-haired, not identifiable as Negro. Audrey's mother is light-skinned and her mother's cousins could and—at least in one instance—have passed for white. In that instance, the mother's cousin bought a house in a white area where her husband would not have been able to. The photo album is also filled with pictures of the many white friends, classmates, even dating partners that John and Audrey have had over the years. Indeed, every such photo album of a Negro in the North records its own story of acceptance or rejection.

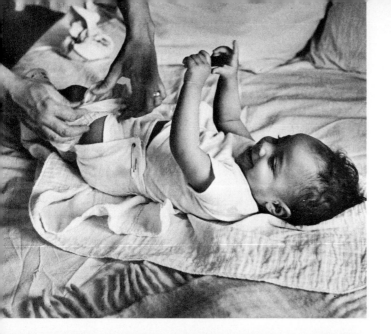

As the Creary children grow up in a black-and-white world, they must also develop a personal mechanism to handle the setbacks facing them. They will be rejected at times only because of their color and at other times it will be difficult to determine whether "it was because . . . OR BE-CAUSE." They will need a high threshold of social and psychological pain, for the uncertainty that still surrounds their parents will not disappear during the next generation. Neither will rebuffs, obstinate prejudice, and bigotry.

Their father, in particular, has learned to smother the constant uncertainty surrounding a middle-class Negro who leaves his ghetto in America. Somewhere below his level of consciousness, awareness of the constant threat of rejection is kept out of sight. John does not permit the awareness to embitter and obsess him. When prodded and probed, when asked the inevitable and recurrent questions about life as an American Negro, his answers convincingly focus on his role as an American, as a teacher, as a Christian, as a father. He talks of "one-to-one" relationships, not of "them" and "us."

This is John's way out of "a life laid waste by a single idea"—to use Colette's phrase when she once asked a successful French politician if he could conceive of such a life. He told the famous writer that he could, for he was lame and was conscious of it almost every hour of his life. It is impossible to guess how many Negroes suffer such a waste in their consciousness of prejudice, and it would be unrealistic to underestimate the context that makes such waste understandable. But both John and Audrey are striving to avoid that waste in their own lives and in the lives of their children. Certainly, more Northern Negroes than ever are succeeding in such an effort.

With their children, John and Audrey strive—as any other middle-class couple—to develop motivation and ambition. They supervise their goings and comings, make certain they do their homework, and bring home acceptable grades. There is also the atmosphere of a stable home where husband and wife share love and respect for each other.

But there is also concern, particularly on the part of Audrey, about the quality of schooling within Harlem and its effect on the future chances of the children. On the other hand, Marianne, whose school is outside Harlem, has her temperamental moments. For a Negro parent it can be difficult to tell whether these are growing pains or the result of her ambiguous footing in a white and in a Negro world. And of the boys, how long can they be shielded from the taint of Harlem?

The Crearys, again like any other middle-class family, are unwilling to remain in a debased urban area when it threatens their family life. Whatever they feel about the debate on whether to strengthen community life within Harlem or shatter the ghetto, the Crearys are unwilling to gamble with Harlem's impact on their children. So far, within their tightly knit family and their self-contained way of life, the Crearys are succeeding in their goals as parents, but John sets forth the need to escape physically from Harlem:

"Our aspirations as a family that can leave are to leave ultimately. We want to get out of the situation. We have a standard of judging what is the best possible—the good life and how better to raise a family. In these surroundings, it becomes increasingly difficult with the size family that we have to provide a home atmosphere. Apartment living is fine if you don't have a large family, and it becomes increasingly difficult in an area where the cultural level is relatively low—where the opportunity and horizons are narrowed."

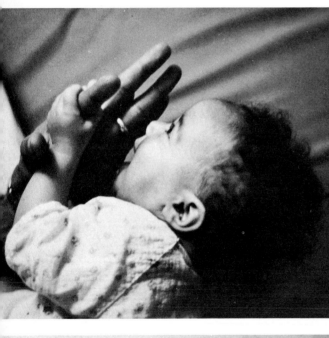
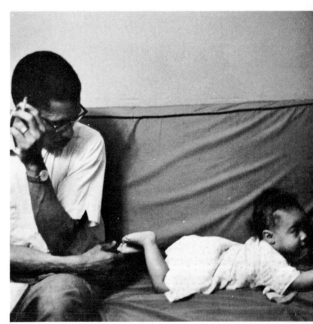
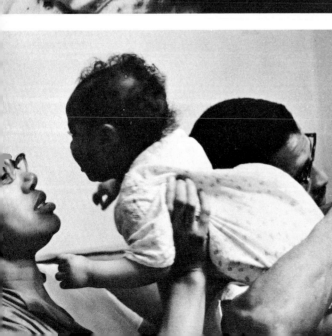
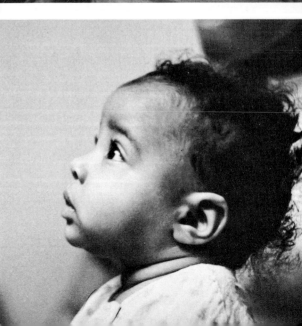

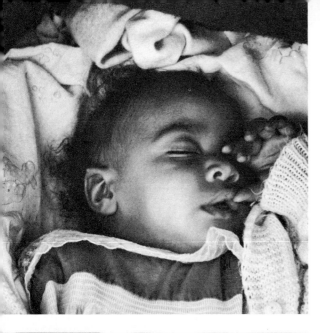

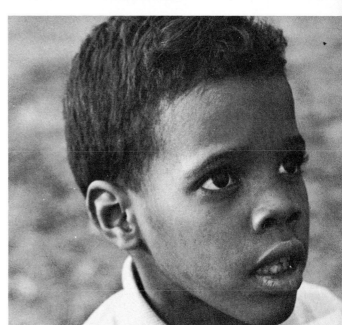

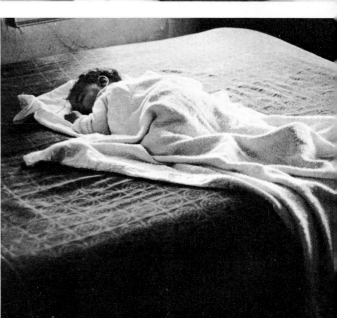

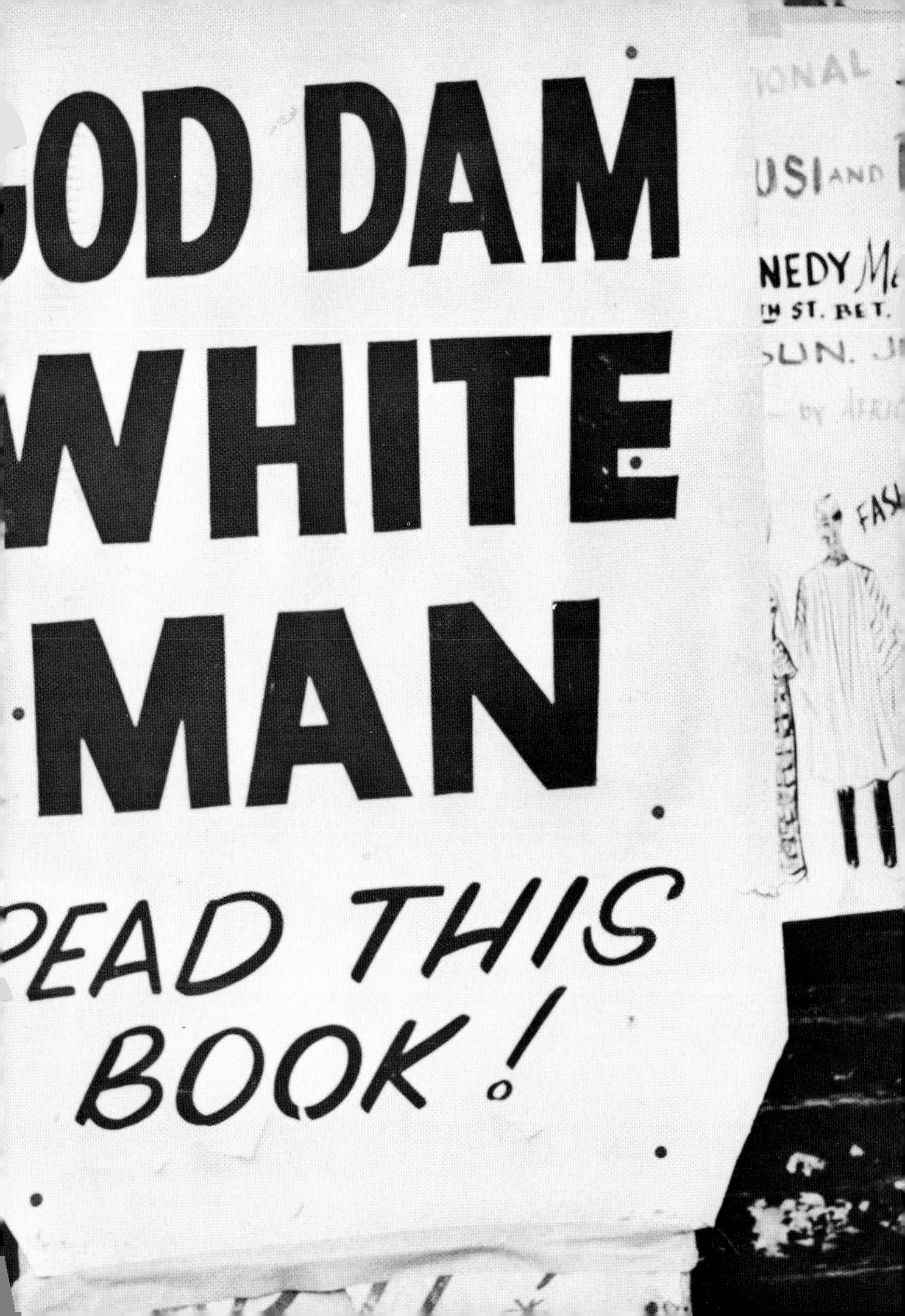
OD DAM
WHITE
MAN
EAD THIS
BOOK!
IONAL
USI AND
NEDY
ST. BET.
SUN.

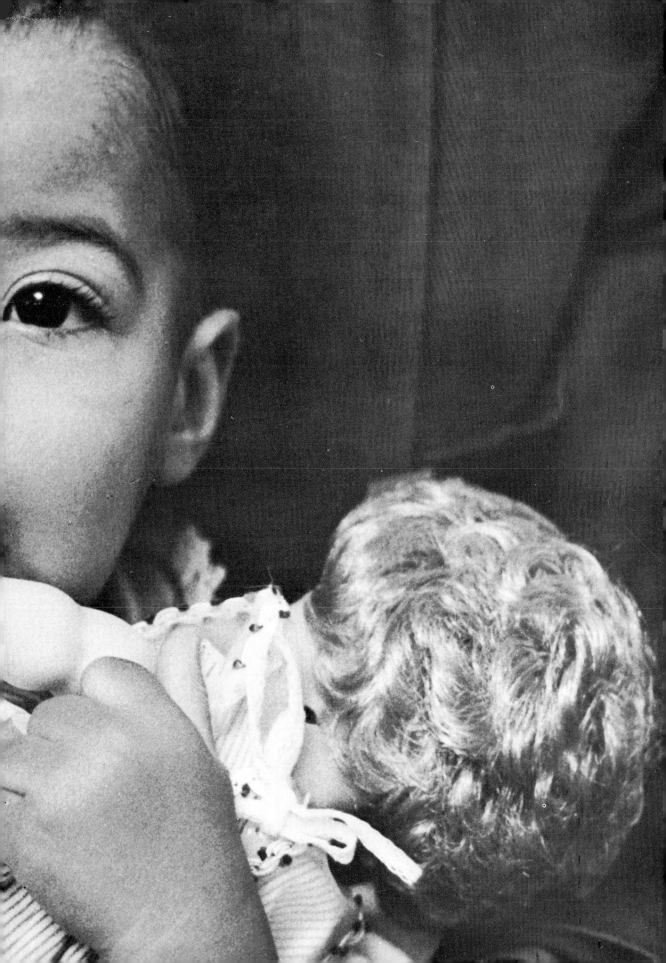

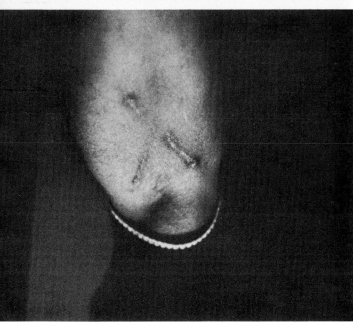

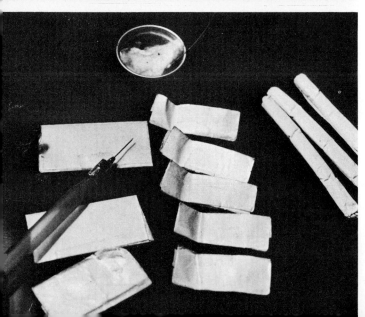

Meanwhile, in the fortress of the home, the Crearys work hard on character training. John sounds like teacher as well as father when he describes his approach: "There is satisfaction in having done something well, the best that you know how, to improve what you have done, to see if you can really better yourself, to go one up on yourself. With the children, I don't show complete satisfaction with what they do. There is always so much more room for improvement. It's not to pick apart what they've done, but to help them to learn to be constructively self-critical. It's an attitude. It doesn't always work. It is something that is a matter of training and growth." While most Negro families are not as well endowed as the Crearys in income, occupation, and education, similar strivings are taking place in ghettoes throughout America. It is another kind of immigrant story, with American Negroes finally finding some of the opportunity that awaited the foreign-born whites who came to the New World for their sake and for the sake of the next generation.

Because the Crearys are well educated, articulate, and highly committed, their philosophy of life and their hopes for the future are well defined. John wants the children to "become persons in the fullest sense, well developed to the maximum of whatever they can be as individuals." Then he continues, framing the words slowly as in a final testament:

"They are unique in their human nature, one by one. They have a priceless gift of being. This is something they will also come to find out just by developing to the fullest extent possible every single potential that they've got. What we hope for them is that they become and remain persons who have an insight into life as it is here and who have a total vision of what their destiny is as human beings. It is beyond living here and now—this is their testing period, their trial period, their time to grow, to find God. We want them to evaluate whatever they are and whatever they meet with in life, judge, choose it freely, and pick the better part. That is putting it in its philosophical sense."

For Audrey, the housewife absorbed in her household, the view is less philosophical. Although she shares John's commitments, Audrey views the children without referring to generalities. College is her hope for all the children, including the girls, and she hopes all will finish their education before marrying. Audrey notes that the children take it for granted that they will go to college, as did their parents. Once the children have their education, they can stand on their own feet, and that is the passport to acceptance and self-reliance that Audrey wants to make certain they have.

Late one evening, as the Crearys reflected on their children and the future, there was a momentary silence. We realized that we were sharing a common feeling. It was a profound sense of uncertainty—about life itself, about each man's ability to cope with it, and about the added uncertainty facing Negro parents. The Crearys are gambling on a future that they cannot guarantee for their children. Part of the gamble is shared by all parents who look at their children and wonder about their future. But a Negro parent also wonders what changes will take place in the coming years and how his child will react to them. Only tomorrow will tell for the Creary children and, at that moment, we stood helpless at the edge of a cliff, unable to imagine tomorrow.